MW00592589

A Tall,
Serious Girl

A Tall, Serious Girl

SELECTED POEMS: 1957–2000

GEORGE STANLEY

EDITED BY KEVIN DAVIES
AND LARRY FAGIN

 QUA BOOKS

Copyright © 2003 by George Stanley

All rights reserved.
No part of this book may be reproduced in any form
without written permission from the author.

Some of these poems have previously appeared in *At Andy's* (2000, New Star Books),
Gentle Northern Summer (1995, New Star Books), *Opening Day* (1983, Oolichan Books),
The Stick (1974, Talonbooks), and *You* (1974, New Star Books);
the editors are grateful for permission to reprint them.

Library of Congress Control Number:
2002094674

TRADE EDITION:
ISBN 0-9708763-2-7

SPECIAL EDITION:
ISBN 0-9708763-3-5

Printed in the USA

Jacket Painting: *Eye on the Sea* by Fran Herndon (2001)
Book Design: Deirdre Kovac
Series Design: Elizabeth DiPalma/DiPalma Design

Published by Qua Books
211 Conanicus Avenue
Jamestown, Rhode Island 02835

www.quabooks.com

EDITORS
Michael Gizzi
Craig Watson

Contents

Editors' Note

This book has emerged partly from a certain frustration experienced by its editors. The Canada–U.S. border, though long and notoriously undefended, is real. When George Stanley (then age thirty-seven, but so youthful-looking that he was often mistaken for a draft dodger) crossed it in 1971, he all but disappeared from American literary surveillance. Though he maintained contact with his friends in northern California, and though more than a few Americans collected his limited-edition books and photocopied manuscripts, Stanley's work has been, in effect, excluded from the canon of "vanguard" American poetry, and from the odd process by which the poems of a small percentage of poets become accessible in the wider world of classrooms and far-flung literary scenes. Though Stanley's recent volumes, issued by Vancouver's excellent New Star Books, are distributed south of the aforementioned border, too often, in our discussions with American poets young and old, we found mention of Stanley's work met with near-total ignorance. Stanley had been inexplicably omitted from Donald M. Allen's *The New American Poetry* (1960), and thus lacked the glamour of that association. And like his mentor, Jack Spicer, Stanley was possibly suspicious of the kind of minor fame that might lead to publication in more established literary journals. Whatever the causes of his obscurity in these States, this selection is offered as a first attempt to situate Stanley's work in relation to that of his teachers (Spicer, Robert Duncan, Louis Zukofsky, Charles Olson), his contemporaries, and the formations, arguments, and poetry that have followed them.

The arrangement of the poems is chronological, though not rigidly so. One of the main objectives of the book is to bring back into print much of Stanley's early work. We also introduce poems that have escaped publication entirely. We have made significant but less exhaustive selections from Stanley's most recent books, *Gentle Northern Summer* and *At Andy's*, both of which are still available from New Star.

Briefly, a few facts and a little context: George Stanley was born into an Irish-American family in 1934 in San Francisco. He was educated there by Jesuits, who are perhaps to some extent responsible for the rhetorical sophistication of much of his early verse, not to mention the frequent religious and classical tropes and figures. As a young man he became part of the poetry "circle" around Spicer, whose influence on Stanley was profound but by no means definitive. After a brief sojourn in New York in 1960 and '61, which brought him welcome contact with such poets as LeRoi Jones (later Amiri Baraka) and Joel Oppenheimer, Stanley returned to the Bay Area, where his peers included poets Stan Persky, Joanne Kyger, and Harold Dull, and painters Russell FitzGerald, Tom Field, and Paul Alexander. The older poets Robert Duncan and Robin Blaser also figured prominently in this milieu. After Spicer's death in 1965, and the subsequent disintegration of the Spicer circle, Stanley migrated to Vancouver, preceded there by Blaser and Persky. He moved again in 1976, this time five hundred miles north to Terrace, B.C., where he was hired to teach English at the local community college, his first academic job. This move, as we believe will be obvious to anyone who reads the poems of this period (which begin with "Mountains and Air"), effected both crisis and change in his poetic practice. It also gave him a clear sense of where he was. "I had absolutely no concept of Canada and didn't get one until moving to Terrace," Stanley tells us. He became a citizen of Canada and returned to live in Vancouver in 1991, where he has since taught at Capilano College. At some point, he also became a citizen of Ireland, which he visits regularly.

It is not our purpose in this note to offer a brief for the artistry and relevance of Stanley's verse. The poems themselves do that, and clearly enough invite response and analysis. Stanley is an American-Canadian-Irish poet whose work is marked in a variety of ways by the history of his age, whose skills are obvious but never merely indulged as such, and whose range of reference – deserts, mountains, cities, friends, memory, love, lovers, political resistance, gay liberation, the North, frontier resource rip-offs, American legend, Canadian argument, Irish repartee, and the terrors of mortality – is, to say the least, considerable. He is also, often, extremely funny – one could speak of the *hilarity* of mortality. And he is still very much at work, having lately begun an epic (*Vancouver*) that owes something to Williams's *Paterson* and a lot to the pleasures and absurdities of his adopted hometown.

A note on orthography: Stanley's emigration north is signaled in the text by a switch from American to Canadian spelling. All other deviations from whatever standard one imagines exists reflect authorial intention.

K.D. and L.F.
September 11, 2002

A Tall,
Serious Girl

Pablito at the Corrida

Instance found him bronzing
in the fat veal country
whittling on reeds

and brought him on this suddenly silent stage,
his hungry knees cried underneath
the gilded starch, the little hands
inside could hardly make his brain
look here, look here,

then the cold horn elbowed through gasping pain
to the secret eggs of him
and the stone crowd stood up and bawled.

Now the brothers read lauds in Spain,
raped on the shining sand
his leatherette heart pours out
its criminal cache
of strawberry powder.

Power
is an act of the many, to
Pablito in the elephantine dusk
Christ was a power leaping on the wall.

Would power only sleep in the blue steel,
obedient as Christian Africa,
or crack from A to B for him,
but alas, it bowled from the bull,
came off the feverish mob for his kill,
now cordons of ants would like to remove his brain.

Let the judgment of headlines fall on him then,
let the hack eulogist with lead slug
stamp his human wax into bloodless grace,
will anyone blame anyone for the lie?

Pompeii

When I read this poem I think of Pompeii.

When they dug up Pompeii the poems were gone,
flower-like and fragile in the stone,
giving nothing to the stone,
honey alloyed to the stone,
making nothing sweet.

The eyes of the matrons burned on the dark blue walls,
under their eyes in shallow pools,
the bell of a xylophone, silver,
bell of an ambulance,
bell of a burglar alarm,
a trying to watch the slowest of motion,
a grinding explosion,
change everything in the complexity of a second.

When I read this poem I know Pompeii is at hand.

They were unready. It came at the wrong
hour for them, the silver bell.
Some little dignity argued a minute with the enclosing,
and all that was left then was the gesture,
virginity, the little lost dog come home
leaping and leaping caught as in a cartoon.

When I read this poem I know Pompeii is imminent,
I know we are moving easily into frenzy,
I feel like taking off my hat to Pompeii
before running.

•

I should talk like the elder Pliny
until I die and then like the younger
reporting my own death:

                    I was too tired
to go see the eruption. Besides,
Uncle had set me a reading in Cicero.
I read it. I bathed and took dinner.
My uncle died there with a silly cocked hat
on his head like a real admiral. When the wind
changed sparks began to fall. Mother and I
went north. I had to carry her.
Now it is beautiful weather.
I am still reading. Cicero's style
is most Roman of all.
                    Dear Tacitus,
my uncle died there,
he died stoically I am told,
all his debts were paid,
Mother and I are well.

My dear Pliny, they were such
nice people, the dead.

                    •

We are moving so easily into frenzy,
with never a backward glance, so graciously,
the silver bell will ring in the afternoon,
bell of a xylophone,
bell of an ambulance,
bell of a burglar alarm,

and Pompeii, the dull unconscious lurch
exploding under the bay.

We will be prepared, but unready.
Speech will be on our lips then,
light winged, watching the light flame
flowing under your flesh, translucent,
becoming conscious of
the dark flame, the dark red
wall collapsing behind the flying soot,
and your two white hands are
shriveled to black twigs,
unable to say,
gesturing bone.

What it is you were going to say
will remain unsaid, even the flattening
words will ripple in pools of stone
and die between our lips in the hardening hill.

●

There was a time for consolation
in the morning of the state, you and me, Republicans,
read, "The unexamined life is not worth living."
That could console us. But now we cannot
get consolation from Greek maxims
when everybody is licking his lips, expectant.

●

Bell of a xylophone,
Bell of an ambulance,
Bell of a burglar alarm, silver.
Now time has fallen into our hands
out of all the clocks. You look to me
for consolation, and the hot wind
pours by unconcerned, flushing our steepled faces,
and the thick flow of death winnows down the window like grass.

Flowers

In a world of flowers
the enclosing is pregnant with silent clockwork
and the shade with death,
nothing expires with more exhaling of life,
nothing clogs so quickly as sweetness,
nothing turns and burns the unshod foot
so readily, ruinously as
the corruption of petals becoming
conception in the earth. What word
can stifle as well as jasmine in the throat
or unsex in the thrust as sudden as gardenias?
What rash can rush in the flesh contagious as the rose?
Nothing so perpetuates itself dying more stoically,
nothing leaves less taint,

and their death is a lime bleeding,
a green file announcing,
the steel bar in a shot of gin reminding,
anything cold and cold-poured on the nape of the neck,
metallic, lying as prone as flowers in flowers
on the huge steel unwintered earth surrounding
the undying progress of the social worm,

all death is denying a purpose and watching a wall,
and flowers deny their purpose in pantomime,
dying to prove the syllogism,
whatever dies without reason is beautiful,
whatever dies without ransom,
they die without reason and are beautiful,
irreproachable,

once in a violet spring,
illumined by the throat of a dawn gale pouring silver
from the dark blue crooks of an omega,
in a cracking thunder-strewn thaw when the wild
flowers poured out of the slush like crimson lava,
you asked me how they grew,
does something underneath
care enough for flowers to push them up? I said no,
nothing under this sweet green earth
pushes them up. Nothing does.
Flowers were in the air, green and tentative,
tendrils curling uncoiled out of a dead man's nose,
burned on the yesterdays of food.
How do they grow, you asked. I said
one leans on the other's shoulder.

How do they die? Without reason,
hand in hand dying, curtseying just once.
And how do my bare feet come to know the death of flowers?
The idiotic white joy of concrete
poured on them makes no difference. Even then
the last juice winds upward once and sears
everything it finds with mortality and the willingness to die.

2

In a rational poem
written by the unwounded
he is found out by the unsounded speech, irrational,
   in the pig's belly,
the worm is eternally trying,
                        in infected meat,

your death is white and grainy,
                                in modern poems,
the transparent snake is coiled around
the word, sterility in his fangs,
                                in life,
the flowers do nothing but happen,
                                in creation,
there is an earth mother, or goddess, unavenged,
                                        in syllogisms,
the end is contained in the promise,
                                in action,
the hand is stayed by the dream,
                                in bed,
the hand is stayed by the dream,
                                on us,
Texas can come as soon as Pompeii
and more slyly.

            In a world of flowers
no one survives but the one who will grow
like flowers, leaning with Texas
and rising through the balking roar
and webs of madness in the shaft
of the great nomadic wind funnel
into perfect silence and unequalled light,
a rose,
        the Pompeiians are all 21, their eyes wide open,
with the blue bell throbbing merciless underneath,
their curse is built in repetitive font on lead,
they don't need anyone to tell them
how deep these grow,
how deep these flowers need,

no one needs to tell them
one leans on the other's shoulder.

3

And there are flowers in the wainscoting
under lead, and the shade of lead, blanching,
Private R., serologist of New Hampshire, tossing your
   hyacinth head and olive eyes for the grey coffee ladies
   at Little Rock,
Private E., coughing on your ulcer in
   the liver and cream abuse of Bethesda,
Corporal J., slipping fillings out of the
   dental lab, smiling with your mouth full, that could
   not make your head into something to play as long or
   as loud as the loose-strung calliope at Seven Hearts, or
   your bed into safety, wherever,
lying on a GI blanket in Malvern when the beat-up Dodge
   came out of a forest or dream of forest lit up like a
   switch engine and crashed on the embankment, and
   the woman looked up at you out of the spider-webbed
   safety glass with half of her face, whose sister you
   later married,
smashing full bottles of Falstaff on Central Avenue outside
   the Flamingo,
tearing open the damask in the Ohio Club with your tiny
   hands,
coming into my bed and demanding all my chit books,
   getting them,
borrowing my tooth paste, sleeping then later with
   Christine P.,

insisting in the Silver Dollar Cafe that your mother loved
   you more than mine loved me and your dad was more
   cruel,
writing to me finally six times from Tennessee until you
   coaxed out the last dark heavy drop of love the Texas
   sand had not yet robbed and sucked it back into your
   white spider belly airmail from the Brazos, and
   thumbed the seven miles to Fort Campbell singing,
   copper candy imperishable flowers in your
   head,
         Corporal,
what did you ever do for me
but fill my gender with the dying kind,
give me the taste of death apples for Christmas,
and as you left the room that was now a room
point out the sweating angels on the walls,

and name for me the syllogistic dance of flowers,
and point to the heavy numerology of perfection in the stars,
as it scattered, unbanded of purpose, and poured
numbers endlessly on Arkansas,

and name for me the stages of our decay?

I have heard no speech but that of these flowers,
so how can I write in a poem
the whole beginning torment, inching
in the unwindowed passages of the womb.
and muttering "unavenged" under its breath?
Death throws her bitter juice into your eyes,
laughing and preening herself behind the acacia,
giggling death is an idiom of speech,

death is responsible for men
plugging the holes with anecdotes,
talking faster to rethread the lifeline,
unable to stop the syllogism,
an unquenchable flame in your pants,
an imperishable flower, however fierce,
whatever lives to a purpose grows ugly,
you live to a purpose,
you grow ugly,
                and I am already irrevocably ugly
behind the blinders and the new soft face,
Corporal, Pablito.

4

In the blind room,
in Pablito's deathbed,
where the stained waxy hands of Jesus Christ
writhe on the wall, Christ that was a power
in the blind light,
in the arguing out of purpose that robs Pablito of his flowering,
that makes him a pawn for the city desk in Madrid,
that makes him a human-interest death for Reuters,
that consigns his blood to the filthy flowers of posters,
that reminds him to girls,
in the silence of our mothers,
in the cessation of loud tears,
in the cemetery of envisioned memorials,
in the steady bleeding of Pablito,
flowers are the only lives that begin to grow,
flowers that fly newborn and winged as moths
from our dying flesh in the black rain on US 5,

when the forge at Chicago where we warmed our hands goes out for a factory,
and the cities despair, one by one across the continent,
in the dull clank of robots,
in the metal breeding of sanitary beetles
in the hollow thumping underneath the land,
we are on the road.

                In the death of the creating woman
at her crest, the leaf goddess, whose diminishing throb
becomes inaudible under the scream of the new subway
from the heart to the grave,
                    in the twentieth century,
coming on the dead we bury them under flowers
with our tears descending and dissolving
every offering, every headstone melting,
we slice the lime and cover up their eyes,
nothing can stop the burning,
nothing can stop the smallness of our hearts.

The land freighters rush down the concrete bend,
down the inclined land to morning,
hooting to morning cities, Los Angeles, Denver,
their headlights mercy, and we grab a ride.

And the dead lie down under flowers.

This is the elegy I have written for you.
The dead lie down under flowers,
yet I hand you this through thin loam under flowers, dampening,
while the new galling rain is still mordant in our eyes,
but the drop is heavy, poised, ripe with its gift, swelling,
and we will never stop our dying.

Flesh Eating Poem

Nana, Nana, ready for supper?
Pull down the shade.
Cornmeal mush, Nana, cornmeal, really?
Pull down the shade.
I'm a good boy and I've done all my homework.
Yes, Nana, all those books are mine.
Yes, they have always been very friendly.
But the pigeon is slapping his fucking
Wing on the window. Pull down the shade.

The books are friendly but have terrible minds of their own.
It is four miles to someone's room who is never at home,
Or if is wants to talk about Christ and the power of grace
And it's four miles back, and you have to ride the N car.
And transfer? To the 22 bus.
That comes never? Always and always is raining.
And Negroes? Of course there are Negroes.

Pull down the shade.
You should all know what I am doing.
Why would the boys never let me drink beer at their table?
Let me play spaceman? I was a good boy. I did all my homework.
I tried out for shortstop. I would have been an attorney.

But for the cornmeal mush on the wall,
For the cornmeal mush for which Mother will hate me.
She does already? Nana, you sloppy bitch,
Get down on your hard yellow knees with your hard noble heart
And wash up the mush. On the wall, Nana? Mush on the wall?
You want me to look at the wall?
At my little black mother way up on the wall
Like a sticky old spider washing away the mush
With her tears, getting smaller and smaller?

Off there with my serum, Nana, hands off, d'ye hear?
That takes the place of the moon and the inbred power
To change. What did you think when you set the assignment
Two days after the last full moon? The last was the 14th, a Sunday.
Don't look at your calendar! But pull down the shade.
We were here on the 16th, a Tuesday. You thought I'd come back
With my wet weak eyes wide open and waving the same white skin.

What I did with my serum! It did I drink.
I walked past the church. The saints were all
Holding in purple. The deaf old priest
Was hollering at my mother. It was
The feast of the festering wounds.
There were six silver suns in the sky,
The hair matting up clumsily under my trousers,
The nails arching down from my . . . up sprang a boy
From the sand! He said, "Nossir,
Because you wear sandals,
Because you drink at the Hayloft,
Because you eat wax babies. Don't bug me."
I took him up in my arms and began with my teeth.
As full as I could. I clogged and I had to spit out.
Now clean up the mush. Fire Nana. Pull up the shade.

The Fifth Circle of Hell

In the 5th Circle,
in Chavez Ravine,
The ball takes a bad ^{good} bounce.

In the 5th Circle,
It is 1st base on an error,
And the Umpire takes the ball out of his pocket and says
Les' see now, center field oughta be *right there*,
And throws it out into the mud that sucks up and boils
Out of the torments of the damned who suffer in the 5th Circle.

Baseball players,
Poison pen artists,
Weight lifters,
Those who claim to 10 years of youth,
Dealers in masterpieces,
Bloody impulses,
Interrupters of the process,
That Coleridge with his spiked shoe upraised spikes,
As they come sliding into 2nd base,
As they all come sliding into 2nd base,
Traffickers,
Agents,
Those picnickers that left the field
Lousy with their paper cups
And second-rate toothpaste,
Those people with Nevada license plates
And loud cap guns,
As they all come sliding into 2nd base,
And Coleridge lifts up his spiked shoe and
Ty Cobb beside him lifts up his spiked shoe

In the 5th Circle,
In the 5th Circle of Hell that is not Los Angeles.

Tete Rouge

Tete Rouge is the only really important character.

Granted that General Kearney did whatever he was supposed to do and there is an ah ah ah what was it? he arrived on time. I mean all his wagons were in order that is the Mexican bullets did not go thru any of his corn or any of the women sitting on his boxes of corn since they always brought women – where? or whatever they were supposed to be doing – but went with a steady ah ah a steady ah ah ah thru the hearts of his men.

Granted that – what was it? oh yes they were outnumbered – five to one – that the Mexicans are outranked by the Indians in any system of values – except for the savage Arapahoe who had no system of values discernible – and the Indians by the Whites.

Granted that – all arrows pointing towards a somewhat insignificant depression in the Southwestern dust.

And many other Granted Thats – Granted That on the South Fork of the Platte – and Granted That a cabin snowed in were found three skulls – racially identifiable – and enough deadness of fingers for years.

And many others and all sites where campsites burned out a slight char on the prairie – and all X's on maps – and all dotted lines that are easily lost in shifting green and brown contours – despite all that.

It was the French who Colonized the West.

And Tete Rouge is the only really important character.

Now who is Tete Rouge?

Well first of all get it thru your heads the French – or rather the Canadians as they called themselves were always five miles West – that is – they were always to be met coming from the place where no one had been – that is no English or American – I mean the French wd be fucking a squaw and then he wd fuck a brave and then he wd very calmly get up out of bed and go to the door and this in the middle of winter they cd resist since this also is a French invention the others only having invented the equipment for it – right to the door mind you and open it and there wd be all kinds of snow and places where no one had ever been and right out of it came an elk to be shot. So this was how the winters grew so long. And what did the English and the American do?

Well one wd lift the heavy end of the log on his shoulder and the other wd lift the light end and the English wd say now come on now you bloody Yankee bastid take account for the leverage – and so the American he wd move in closer to this imaginary point of balance that is he wd take more of the log on his shoulder and the English wd say come on now move out you bloody Yankee bastid take account of the leverage and the American wd move out farther from this point of balance and this was to lift the log which wd eventually be used for fortification or for shelter of privacy which were hard to distinguish and this wd go on for months and months while the French was laughing and fucking and throwing down more and more of the winter into the valley.

The process of piling up this snow was called Manifest Destiny and the method of making progress that is when the English and the American wd walk hand in hand thru the valleys made by this snow that was called Protective Coloration and the place they had left now log by log they had lifted and that was not now either home or habit and it was called a Granted That. And as the English and the American went farther and farther West and as the Granted Thats were abandoned and the winters grew they eventually got to Oregon which is a country of no seasons since it has no mountains in front of it for the French to fuck on.

54 40 or fight is that they had it out and the things that resulted in this fray are called the Unguarded Frontier – Peaceful Arbitration of Disputes – Lumber and Timber – Common Sense and the Totem Culture – Reptiles and Easy Riders and Fog.

But it was still towards that depression in the Southwest towards which all arrows pointed somewhere near where the S P takes off from Tucumcari I mean the Santa Fe and it is all cactus overgrown keeping their distances and the sand is many colors where the buffalo Indians Mexicans Whites and all that were scared off the mountains by the French came to the great Granted That – well who is Tete Rouge and why is he so important?

Well here are some facts abt Tete Rouge set down in order and you can judge from them altho eventually numberous and lengthy apogees will be made in elucidation who Tete Rouge is.

No. 1 is that whenever Tete Rouge wd ride a horse he wd wear a huge black military cape inside out.

And No. 2 is that Tete Rouge never rode a horse at all since from starting out from the great Granted That in the Southwest he cdnt get on it but when he finally got his foot in the stirrup and rested most of his weight on it and the English and the American took off their hats in the sun and scratched their heads and said well what is it? is he going to go to sleep there? because he didnt make any move to bring his other leg up the whole horse buckled and collapsed and died.

And No. 3 is that whenever Tete Rouge caught sight of a band of Mormons camping around their fire and discussing theological questions he wd ride full gallop up on that camp cape flying and rein up and give a terrific shout of Camp Ahoy! which wd so terrify those Mormons that they would immediately grab huge pots of steaming coffee off the fire and drink them down and fall into an instantaneous and selfish sleep.

And No. 4 is that whenever Tete Rouge caught sight of an eagle he wd ride off and be gone for hours or perhaps days and then to unpatriotically reappear and announce in a sneering and fawning voice that he had killed the American Bird.

And No. 5 is that whenever the party wd encamp Tete Rouge wd upon dismounting from his horse and respectfully addressing the American and English in various Indian tongues and varieties of Creole and Jamaican dialect which wd fitfully enrage them disappear around the back of the piled up supplies and eat all the bread and tear up all the tobacco and lose all the knives.

And No. 6 is that at dinner that night Tete Rouge wd complain that the meat was unsalted and then respectfully demand bread and tobacco and a knife to cut them with.

And No. 7 is that Tete Rouge was the only member of the party who did not at some time contact leukemia or dysentery or sleeping sickness or the ire of the French or perverse love or a passion for fireworks or cramp or Indian legends or nomenclature or morality or acorns but wd sit around all night telling jokes at his own expense and describing the bodies of the first ladies of the eight most populous Southron states until the English and American got up and stomped around in the mist and stumbled around in ravines and fell down and got up and staggered back and met each other at the campsite and pulled out their pistols and fired great aimless rounds of shot at each other with cries of despairing love and kerchiefs tied around their necks and were unable at morning either to shave or to tie the supplies on to the mules because their fingers were so weak.

Now these are facts abt Tete Rouge and abt how the English and American were led to believe they had Colonized the West and eventually learned a little abt botany and microbotany and lectured for the remainder of their lives on these subjects – interspersing these lectures with canny and confidential anecdotes of the Dacotah the Arapahoe the Snake the Kanzas the Ogillallah the Blackfoot the Camanche the Root Digger and the Sioux.

But why is Tete Rouge and who is Tete Rouge and who really Colonized the West?

Well it is not really audible what was said that the French or the Canadians as they called themselves or while the bullets went thru General Kearney's men with an ah ah ah and while the drunken officers yelled Fall Back the absolutely blind drunk private yelled Forward Boys Forward they defeated the Mexicans even capturing the carts of rope they had brought to war for tying up the Norteamericanos on the evening of that day when sombreros wd fly in the air and the Mexican flag be planted in Evansville with a yi – they cd not have done all that so far from world conflict and valor up there in the snow so solemnly fucking the ugly dark girl then the lonely dark boy then making that coffee by the receipt of Voltaire hot as hell sweet as a woman black as night strong as the will never. The French have one serious fault. They imagine they are Indians. Any one who wants to be understood shd go to France. I mean they still walk around that way with bones in their nose saying How How How like F P sd the Indian signified half the emotions of which he was capable. How How How up and down those crooked streets reading those bilingual newspapers (I mean Montreal of course not France) not caring a bit for the real Canadiens with an E (except when Richard slashes somebody in the face with his skate they go out and collect the francs to pay the fine taking them to the Exchange Bank to change into bankers dollars they go How How How all the way up to the Commander's Office) How How How at night remembering how cold it was when they fucked something hot how light she felt to fuck something dark in the snow. The Americans gave them the automatic die press stamper in Exchange. But inventing winter is not the same as Colonizing the West so who was it?

Well one day this old theatrical trunk with silver fittings and beat up dusty leather snapped open way out in one of those snowed in Granted Thats up in the mountains and out jumps this roly poly red head boy in a green serge coat with a knife between his teeth. Well who are you says Boisverd the Trapper turning over in bed away from something dark and ripply or Qui est vous? and this fellow takes the knife and flings it eight feet across the cabin into the wall. Blank Blank Blank he sd and those blanks stand for his name since he then sd his name. Now this was an English name or rather a Scotch-English name. It was long and had a capital letter near the middle an M I think and abt eleven letters after that and it ended with a silent one.

Well first of all remember a Frenchman – or rather an Indian as he calls himself when he is inventing winter – especially when turning over in bed from it – and there is an ah ah ah thru something like a fish shaped like his mind. There are maxims. I mean there are rules of conduct. Savoir faire. As the gentleman sd when upon opening the door to his bedroom he found his wife in a Great Heat of Joy with Another Man. Oh Please Continue he sd. Oh By No Means Let My Untimely Arrival he sd. Now Boisverd was used to such civility that is to say the farce – or the comedy without apprehension – was unknown to him. Deep in the pillow the Indian Girl was chuckling. Snow ran down the sides of the Rockies like tears of delirious laughter. How How How sd the Indian Girl – How How How. Tais-toi sd Boisverd. Sacre enfant de garce he sd. How many letters does it have? Eleven – after the M – sd Tete Rouge. Magaral – amalagaloohar – magoilar – it must be Irish sd Boisverd. I cannot pronounce it. It is not Irish sd Tete Rouge. Blank Blank Blank he yelled. He jumped up and he knocked all the boxes off the shelves – the cornmeal on the floor and the flour and the bullets – he jumped up to where the 5 gal can of kerosene he knocked over Boisverd. Blank Blank Blank he yelled. How How How sang the Indian Girl dancing in a cloud of flour. This is how you make winter yelled Tete Rouge. At last we are young she sang and she smiled with her lips expecting her teeth to do the same but they did not. Hip hip hip yelled Tete Rouge. I cannot fire a rifle I cannot shoe a horse I cannot ride 2 miles without becoming fatally overcome with stickleburs! I will Colonize the West! and out he ran into the snow and down the mountain. Take me with you she cried. No he yelled from a great distance. You must stay and be an example to your people.

That is so she sd biting into her finger. Hip hip hip – you cd still hear Tete Rouge bounding falling stumbling down the mountain. Hip hip hip. Now first I must clean up this Granted That she sd. It was lucky she thought of that because only her grabbing for the rag kept her from biting it off. She began to wipe the kerosene off Boisverd and he turned over and sd – Wont you be late for church honey? Absentmindedly she kissed him. You know I can go to evening service she reproved him. When she got to the flour she tried throwing up a few handfuls in the air to see if it wd stay. Hip hip hip yelled Tete Rouge. She picked up all the cornmeal and put it in a big pot and went outside and got some snow and put it in and was abt to boil it to make mush when Boisverd said – I want sausages this morning! You know I always eat sausages on Sunday you dumb bitch. All right she sd and she took some of the wet cornmeal out of the pot and made little turd shaped sausages out of it and put them in a pan to fry. And eggs! sd Boisverd. You know I always eat eggs on Sunday. All right she sd and she took little globs of cornmeal and put them in the pan with the little turd shaped cornmeal sausages and took some snow and made little white wheels around the globs. When they were done she gave them to Boisverd to eat. He spit out the first two or three mouthfuls but after he had finished the rest he sd – That's good. You make the best sausages and eggs in the whole world.

When Tete Rouge got to the great Granted That in the Southwest the American and the English were playing a game with a knife and a lizard out in the compound. Neither one of them had his shirt on and both of them had terrible cases of sunburn. The American and the English were friends primarily because neither of them cd bear to distrust the other. They slept in the same bed – ate their meals together – and to sum it up – in a manner of speaking – they pooled their resources. Neither wd ever cheat the other at games. If the English held the Queen of Spades at Hearts for instance he wd never pass it to the American without passing at the same time at least one low spade – say the five – as a backer for it. And if the American threatened mate at chess he wd always warn the English by saying some such thing as – Well that just might do it – or – Nice – how those bishops back each other up. (The American did occasionally play chess with both bishops on the same color.) Of course he wd never say these things unless mate was certain. But they did – as the English so winningly put it – soften the blow. Theirs was the finest friendship to be found outside the Indian Villages. It is a wonder how they ever got sunburned.

Well the American and the English are playing this game when up rides Tete Rouge. And as soon as the American and the English see Tete Rouge they of course immediately get out their books of botany and microbotany and here is the American sitting in the shade comparing some wild grasses to the photographs and here is the English out in the blazing sun crawling around with his increasing glass and here is a worm or some other segmented thing that is humping itself and falling and making steady and significant progress towards some point or destination or tiny Granted That in the clumps of sun dried clay covering the compound and indeed except for sparse grasses and damp places covering the entire Southwest there are these worms humping themselves and falling making progress toward some previously agreed upon speck a shine of the sun on some faceted grain of sand but here in the compound this green worm or segmented thing making steady progress and the sun overhead making steady progress. Halloa there says Tete Rouge – Who are you and where are you from? What are ya doin and where are ya goin? We are studying botany and microbotany of course say the English and the American. But Tete Rouge has seen the knife and the lizard and immediately his eye lights upon the worm which is rising and falling and making steady but silent progress. General Kearney is not coming he says (how does he say it? ah ah ah go the bullets thru their hearts) as tho he did not intend to say anything at all. What? say the American and the English leaping to their feet. What? No says Tete Rouge. General Kearney is not coming. The Mexican War is over. You had best pack your things and head home.

Now the sun goes down and in the weak light of sundown the American and the English are carrying out of the Granted That all their possessions and it is incredible the amount of possessions they have accumulated in Winning the West. Well there are buffalo hides – and buffalo heads in huge bottles with pickling spices – and then there are the horns of buffalo and the tails – and long lariats made of buffalo guts – and then there are buffalo eyes glazed over for stickpins and buffalo hearts and lungs – and then there are cans of salt pork – and bottles of lettuce – and theatrical trunks full of bread (Hold on now giggles Tete Rouge – thats where I used to live) and then there are steamer trunks – and leather suitcases full of fishes – and boxes – and crates – and mailbags full of chocolates in gold foil – and then there are archery sets and cameras and collections of stamps and portable hives of bees and hills of ants and hats and printed scarves and rifles and microfilm and quilts and diving suits and pressurized oxygen chambers and pickaxes and dynamite – and then come the journals – and the diaries – and cartons and cartons of writing paper – and long into the night they drag out everything and from the corral the English brings the mules and then after them horses and wagons and from behind the Granted That the American comes in the moving van full of springs and mattresses and alarm clocks. And the loading and the tying fast and the stacking go on thruout the early hours while Tete Rouge drinks and dances and sings and lights matches that he has stuck in their boots and climbs drunkenly up on the Granted That waving a candle and once rides out a long way from the Granted That – say two miles – and imitates a coyote. And at sunrise they are ready to go. But they must wait because Tete Rouge has drunk all the coffee and while they are unloading the coffeepot and hotplate (which they plug into the dynamo) and all these things being under the darkest and the deepest mattresses in the moving van – Tete Rouge must tell them the story of how the West was Won. Isn't that peculiar says the English – I seem to have lost my front tooth. Your front tooth? says Tete Rouge as far as I can see all your front teeth are in place. No not my front tooth says the English – my front tooth. The one I yanked out of that Ogillallah skull up on the Platte. Well I certainly dont have it says the American. Well now I didnt say you did now did I says the English. Well youre always blaming me for something says the American. Oh stow it says the English you bloody idiot. Hey there now says Tete Rouge. Oh well I didnt mean it to sound that way says the English. Hip hip hip says Tete Rouge – off with you now. Did you remember to pack my red flannels? says the American. And off they go – the American and the English flags fluttering aimlessly in the wind and a vague little blast of trumpet from abt 500 feet up – say from the South South West.

Now these are stories of Tete Rouge and of the Winning of the West but it is still uncertain how Tete Rouge got his name or for that matter how anything Westron got its name those things having been debated at length in the Marble Halls the name Idaho being at one time simultaneously applied to three states – Idaho being a Snake name meaning talking out of the corner of your mouth. The State of Utah has two lips sd Tete Rouge. One of the things he wd carry with him on his treks was a small pocket telescope which wd greatly diminish the size (when expanded to full length) of any hostile object. This enabled him to proceed on his way in a sanguine and discursive frame of mind but did not greatly increase the rate of his progress. Tete Rouge's own journal of his experiences is of considerable interest. It is written in an extremely spiderish and elongated hand of which the loops of the f's. the p's and the j's drop like snares into the open letters of the next line at times when there are enough letters caught dragging it up into the one above – occasionally by repeated loopings of these loopings dragging up several lines or even an entire page into a heavy and scratchy blot at the top. Pages such as these are often puzzling to professional collectors of Westron lore who seem at times unable to decipher his meanings or unable to contain several undeciphered meanings in their heads while they scratch about in the ink for another or even in their notes which at times exhibit this curious phenomenon of *densing* themselves.

On the whole however his journals are full of delightful and sprightly anecdotes such as I quote May 19 1848 caught sight today of a huge grizzly but as I charged towards it keeping it always in range with my telescope the dark object suddenly split in two – the two halves then flying off in opposite directions – what I had taken for a grizzly at a thousand yards was really two crows perched on a branch at ten – or this Oct 1 1848 the Indians say the White is only a more spirited type of Beaver – or this May 7 1849 this morning passed by a huge and stagnant lake where a great number of fully dressed people were bathing and drinking coffee.

In the spring of 1850 – while traveling thru that state of the 3 eventually to receive the appealation Idaho – there occurs this curious passage – Apr 27 1850 yesterday upon following a trail thru these hitherto unexplored parts it very oddly and for no apparent reason split into two trails – each of exactly half the width of the original. This phenomenon so interested me that I at once resolved to follow both of these trails to their ends. What was my consternation you may imagine when about noon I came upon two forks – in every way identical to the one I had previously encountered except of course that these were the half in size of the first. Persistently I followed the four resultant trails and within 2 or 3 hours found – as you might have expected – four additional forks. As I followed the eight narrow trails thru the late Idaho afternoon they became exceedingly difficult and rocky to the foot – and when by sundown they had split (as gentle reader you have no doubt anticipated my progress by predicting) into sixteen – I had constantly to keep all thoughts from my mind save those of where my foot wd next land. All around these trails were great fields of lush grass and as the evening deepened strange white flowers opened wide their waxy petals and began to vibrate with a peculiar verbosity and odor. Along abt 11 o'clock I reached sixteen difficult and precarious forks. I had intended to follow these trails to the end but being almost overcome both with fatigue and with the heavy and surreptitious odor that crept voicelessly from the flowers I laid myself down to sleep resolving to further pursue them in the morning.

Then I fell asleep but not before it seemed to me (or was I dreaming?) that I caught sight of a large white structure just beyond the farthest visible ridge and heard for an instant a sound as of many people asking the same question at once. But alas – upon waking – all thoughts of my manly intentions had slipped my mind and I recalled them only upon encamping for my noon meal by this pleasant creek some five miles from where I took rest – where I am now writing these notes. To date there has been little note of this passage in the more serious journals of scholarly opinion on these matters – tho in Vol 35 No. 6 of Westron Studies, Professor Ronert of Oregon State suggests Tete Rouge may have been following sheep trails.

Pony Express Riders

The men that fought and loved each other
were a storm,
and the Pony Express Riders
knew this,
and could not forget it.

Almost unable to forget
they rode out. On white
horses they streaked
across a dark land, and one
overtook the other.

Able to forget
they were the men that fought and loved,
they rode.

Ahead of the wind that rose,
ahead of the storm,
ahead of the sound of the storm, into

a wilderness.

The Mountain

Late breezes blow their hair back
as they ride in the afternoon.
A mountain
rises ahead of them.

The horses step
up over dry brush and rock.

They leave
the underbrush behind
and climb the rock. They
plunge up, carrying the riders
through the trees.

The shadows of the trees
fall on the riders.
The light
dies on the branches.
They ride on.
The horses
carry them.

Late at night
they carry them
out of the trees.

The Riders

They ride into town
on white horses,
their manes
gleam in the sun,

past the Saloon
and the State Bank,
past the Hotel
and the Store.

They ride through town
on white horses.
They ride
into the sun.

The Moon

They fried a squirrel in its grease,
ate it with bread and coffee,
laughed and yelled, and their fire
roared, and leaped.

Then they lay down, still laughing.
and talking, and the flames died down
to the stones and they slept
and the embers glowed,
and went out.

Then the moon rose.

At the Edge of the Prairie

Buffalo ran on the prairie.
One rider waited in the trees,
the other rode out. Sun glinted
on the chamber of his rifle as he put
the bullet in it.

Black backs, black charging heads,
feet driving. He rode

even with them, raised his rifle
to his shoulder, and fired.
One fell, the rest ran on.

He got off his horse and went over
to look at it, and the other rider
rode out and got off his horse.

The Girl

In the late sun,
the shadows flew
under the feet
of the horses.

The girl
saw them ride by,
saw one of them
turn.

They rode
till sundown,
and reined up.

All night
he lay
under the stars.

Intermezzo

Riding at dawn on the prairie,
in the morning he came
to a few trees, the watering place,
dismounted and led his horse down
the mud slick to the stream.

Drinking from the stream he saw
his face reflected in it, the trunks
of the trees, the sky,
and the sun, in broken patterns,
fallen leaves, on the water.

He led his horse up from the stream,
mounted, and rode away.
He rode faster now, on the prairie,
in the morning sun, white
streaks on the Rockies gleamed.

Approach of the Storm

Leaves torn from dry branches
      rise in the wind,
birds wheel in a bleak sky,
a pale flash lights the East.

The brown and white cattle
      lift their heads,
the rider reins up, waits.

The storm advances,
　　black clouds torn by
stabs of lightning,
　　the sky
at the horizon darkens,
the rain begins.

A torrent in the dark,
　　the cattle run
for shelter, barns, fences.
　　The rider
rides in the storm.

Death

The horse lay on his side.

Blood continued to flow
from the wound in his flank,
though the arrow
had been removed.

He looked up at the man
with a white eye.
A spasm
passed over all his muscles,
he trembled and sweated, fighting
the pain, and gave
a low cry.

The man knelt by him,
and holding the pistol
to the base of his skull,
he fired.

Evergreens

When he rode up into
the evergreens, they were darker
than the sky an evening star
was faint in –

Snow whirling, snow-
flakes falling, drifted down,
melted on the needles,
and piled up around the trunks.

In deeps and hollows he rode,
in starlight, shining on the white
inclines, the snow-
branches and tips of the highest
evergreens –

On the steep
ridge that led
to the peaks –

The Bear

The whinny of his horse
woke him,
                to snow,
his gear on a branch, the
starry sky.
A twig cracked.

Slowly, he
reached for his gun, and
slowly,
        turned.
The bear's eyes
gleamed.

At gun-
        point,
the bear backed off,
and went
            down
his trail.

Dawn

Light returns to the sky,
a wild radiance
brighter than moon
or star –

The trees are near,
rain on their dark
leaves, dew on
the grasses –

The birds
are awake
in the nests
in the trees –

with his hat
back on his head
and an easy
rein he rides –

on the last hill –
The plains
go on
to sunset.

Immortality

The sky goes round the earth,
the flat white sun comes up.
The Pony Express Riders ride
on the plains.

Indians on horseback
fit arrows to their bows,
arms draw the bowstrings taut,
and the arrows fly!

The Pony Express Riders,
struck by the arrows,
fall from their horses
to the plains.

The Lake

In the desert wind he rides
toward the pale sun
torn in the clouds.

The dead lake lies
on the desert, reflecting the sky,
and reeds at the edge, that thrive
in salt, move in the wind.

                        Then,
his reflection's on the lake,
riding, in the sky.

            Wind
moves the water, the clouds
and tips of the reeds dissolve
to light on the lake.

Largo

In the shadow
of a hill he rides,
his shadow rides the hill.

Rider on a white horse
in sunlight to the line
of blue,
        on a dark horse
in a valley of wild fruit trees,

the gnarled branches bare
and flowering.

In the shadow
of a hill he rides,
his shadow rides the hill.

A Translation for Jeorge

One summer evening I rode out
and the flowers
closed their petals.
All ahead

was dark, no path
in the trees, but as I rode
the trees led me, so to my own
heart it seemed, necessity

led me on through the forest though it darkened,
though the plants that bore the white
and closing flowers gave way
to plants that did not.

It was not
my own heart I was
listening to, there was no
sound.

White Matches

1

One bird called White
pecked with a gold beak.
Another, Black,
becked with a cold pique.

What birds with wings
the color of X-rays fly
Choristers I call
and Christers He –

and each
receives the dawn
in its own place
luminous as a file.

2

I thought you were savage.
Then my mind
was strong and blind.
Witness of me to cloy on

your fitness.
The arms of my legs
wanted you to track
an enemy

face down.
I picked up
the Jack of Hearts
here.

3

At dawn the mosquitoes
eat night, luscious
in their jaws,
perfumed and awed.

They aid without approving of it.
It wouldn't be long.
They reveal the day
buzzing away to the end.

Yawning, I see morning.
I hope the ship is a house,
and the light through the wings believable,
though a saw-blade would be accurater.

4

What graceless guy
kept you dreaming in your cave
until
the first wave went by?

Then you rushed to the cliff's edge
overhanging the sea
and knew he was not what
he was said to be.

I think of this when
I hang up my hat
on the wall and
sit down to eat.

5

The old train goes
where the old train goes
where it does not snows.
The stupid green

the cows eat lean
out to the end of the scene.
Where the sea is heard
there's a lowing herd,

a blurred third.
Let that
rock fall
far.

6

"When he asked me
to go to Europe with him
in the Fall,
there were no strings attached.

But now,
out of two weeks of loneliness
in New Hampshire,
there comes this long white string.

I don't want to go anywhere
as anybody's lover.
I don't even want my pity
to be attached to me."

7

A ball hurted.
I uncrossed my legs
and it still hurted.
How to do this in the taxicab.

I tried to learn for years how good it is.
A victim told me in a voice not mild
he hoped to have his eyes
where the stars were, outside,

and listening to several voices,
If we are at all human we must at least let our voices
listen to us, and he cried.
So then there was a lamp lit for others.

8

Flit in, little fairy,
with no lines of innocence.
Breathing this air of antidotes
I choked on the rare gases.

I could see every leaf I saw,
the landscape was that impractical.
(But when I turned on the light
Dotty said, "You've made it night.")

Ozone, argon, mercury.
At a two- or three-way
junction I sniffed.
It was blurred like photographed traffic.

9

That sense of indefinite longing
that seemed to be at the heart of my life
is gone.
Now I long for what I know.

My life
begins to shorten.
The number
of far expectations possible decreases.

Though the long lives of others
in which I am a moment
lengthen.
I write of this as one involved in a secret.

10

I'm not satisfied with them,
but I'm not going to change them.
And whose public wall is it, anyway,
where dogs piss

lightly,
as if to stain the ground
a kind of romantic yellow?
Whose eyes

I idolize,
whose lips I kiss,
whose pride I bite
with a kind of nobility.

White Matches

White matches
struck on ground glass in glue
made 20 tiny flames to you.
It is called a book,

so they sell it or ask for it.
Gimme 2.
Time is as well contrived
as action (what in a horse is checked)

is not – called headstrong.
Give him his rein!
As out of a novel or over a hedge
that lost its color the steeplechase rider leaped.

12

Simple Simon
met a pieman.
And Simon Pure
met a pieman.

The questions the Simons asked
the piemen had no time for.
"For a penny! For what I can get!" one laughed.
And the other: "I'll see you at the Fair!"

For which Simon, which pieman, read:
So it was that after that long day
of wins and losses
I thought of you.

For Knute Stiles

They would force   scrunched
paler-than-thou   heads   up

     on razor stalks
     against which a beetle might run head on
                   (like a fist)
and the two halves, one
       to the bluebells, one to the fence
       climbers in shadow
                  Then the morning-glory
                  is a hang-up
                  it is too stressed
the hairy foliage outside
            parks and windows

What we dare with commercial products, pasting
         them, one by
a chalked **X**, a love letter, "men are patient"

  and presume
        he will come out of his door-
        yard with a
            collage
        held ten feet out in front   of him

The trumpet has found its place
it is to the lips
        blown clearly

         that song has
         nothing to do with
         getting up in the morning!

But the flower, it would
       bloom underground if it could
          and the whole
evolution
       the head of a monkey

You, Morning-Glory, you have
   no charge on landscape!   you, first act

    your breath
           wintrily in the air, the red door

   swinging on its hinges, the blue
               into the sun

and coming down the street, still,
the man with his painting,
which makes shadows on the pavement,
the feet, the 4 X 8
           oblong

                  which makes
                  different oblongs,
                  and at night

the buildings stand up, and talk
      over our heads.

Punishment

A Sea

The iceberg's arch mirrored
islands in the archspace.
Where the ship, contrary
to clouds, sailed, the bowsprit
slick with frozen rain, the helms-
man saw the bergs that seemed to stay
anchored by their eight-ninths underwater,
the sea to flow, thwarting the warmer current,
and cloudlit islands greenblackly shifting.
They drove toward the pointed and streaming
star, the beams retaining
heat in the hold and light in the cabins,
the deck gleaming in the rain.
And if they passed a berg it seemed
to be a monument of certainty,
a solidified fact that dared them with its prime-
having-been-reached, reproached them
with its pure size and whiteness.
A bell clanged and the shift changed.
The helmsman went back into the square
of orange glare that silently admitted him,
and the new helmsman came to the deck
and the wheel. At 86th St.,
local and express tracks run level.
The express tears through the iron girders.
The local horns and speeds,
local and express jockey in black until
on inclined track ten iron cars accelerate
in flashing local windows an unlit
station's shadowy stairwells and pillars.

2

Language has no face, only hair –
on the brown skull like the word Africa –
honey–vinegar–mustard color –
The wild American pig in the reeds
white circles of echo bleats.
A monkey, answering makes
mocha mistakes. The pith-
helmeted hunter hears –
Nueva York in his pearl-handled ears.
Natives charm the future with their knuckles.
Successive passes lure the quarry in
as no intense love cartridged and triggered.
The safari is at one of its clear rings.
Light later than the sun
burnishes the lower leaves
of snake trees like a Tarnhelm.

3

Unrolling in their thin dark skin like snails on their tails
your eyes glazed yellowishly on this lake –
reflected winter sunlight faceting
the flex and leather of a rider on a narrow
legend in the mind – the snow there bright and near,
resisting the imprint of the horse, as he is riding,
drifting – And the snow is the legend.
Bright and near,
bright and far, the snowy mountains in the lake –
the mirror where the telephone is ringing.

4

Uptown the ten-car train plunges into the lake
with a hiss of steam, in car by car it darkens (I take
the "D" to 59th, the 7th Ave. Express) a his-
s an amber light (if he is right) this
he secretly reads) the red
lights on the local
pinkened in the tunnel to dull reflectors
are dark as garnet-in-the-rough on the trestle
at 125th St. – And the flanged
wheel strikes sun's
sparks from the rails – in sparks
of light, sparks of ice fly –
in ice, mist – and dark where the stars shine
like signals in the tunnel – In local windows –
the man with a lantern and a pickaxe's seen –
In the brightwork the polishing rag fails to brighten
corroded oxides of copper and zinc
island in the luster-streaked friezes
of the crewmen, the signed, striped-
shirted and shanghaied – The man
with a lantern and a pickaxe's seen for-
wardships of the fur-throated British passengers –
in the bright-
work the mottled brighter
streaks are the lighted
cabins, and a dark line the line of the bow –
and a paleness in the brass the arching ice
where rereflected phantasms strike
at the actual radiant expressions.

The Death of Orpheus

Animal grace in others and he
saw though his indifference
rained like hell spaces.
What did he see?
The long, dusty road,
his arms wide things moved
over and under.
The bird, over, the name –
less urge, under, it was hard to see.
Among them danced fellows and maids.
There first he saw as in a dream a toad,
a dying toad in a hollow of not-quite-air-or-water
belch from his thighs a string of bubbles that rose,
on each an aerial rider of least size.
Oh *his?* Yes, for the toad head toad-
eyed and sinking in the slime was crowned
with dark gold but his legs where white and female
Her.
No, he saw lifting his eyes
the first horizon.
Twanged
with his stiff nails the strings
that when those aerial riders grown full size
rushed from that edge of pain,
that horizon, in their rush
seized   and lifted

The sailors in their ship
sailed on. Ice hit the windows
of their cabins
where Determination
sat like a cruel man
with a twitch in his eye.

Oh, we called that a twinkle, we
sailors called that a twinkle,
though we were fed on salt and leather
and our teeth were filled with tungsten,
we called that a twinkle.

A False Start

If I will listen
I will hear you
because the famous song
is short.
        Flowers
where you can't be.
A funeral.
The dogs are vicious
and the children
impatient, or stare
at a piece of jewelry.
All the sexual
is uphill,
        they carry
a piece of stone.
The flowers are examples
of what has been said,
        your head.
That is cocked
            by the sun.
It is down to
            this piece of grass,
                those
eyes.
    The victims
are where something to drink
has gotten cold.
                    Still
You aren't through with them.
Fine, it is fancy, but fancy
is grass, their
grass. It can be used

for parties.
    Whatever you call it,
this has no use. Nor are
the children, children
any more. It is something
for which a man would
shut his eyes, open his ears,
for which the night would be
Spanish.

Jonathan Edwards Poem

Then when
                Jonathan Edwards
turned that heavy head
flared
        his nostrils
from the left
a drop of ink
                fell

"People,"
          he said, "one got
"too big for his britches, another, fat
"too big to get in his own house." "No,"
I said
"tell me how that language got spoken."

Then Jonathan Edwards said,
"it was taught in schools.
"They wrote it on paper,
"Girls
"and boys
                and a kite
                is a blue diamond
                high in the sky
                floating over Massachusetts
                got
                eaten by an ocean-going bird
                down through thousands of feet of air
                the string fell

and Jonathan Edwards said,
"I was smoking a Turkish tobacco

"the fumes
              got up into these books,"
got up to show me some books
"stained the pages, see,
"burned the lines off
"these charts

                    I asked a man
                    in the steam-bath.
                    He was a merchant, when the hurricane
                    blew him downstairs,
                    the raisins exploded
                    the ax
                              rusty
                                        chopped up into
                    some light. Now the grooves
                    in the stone
                                        drip by drip
                    carried away
                                        his fat

and tick, tick
I asked
along the street

and Jonathan Edwards said,
"People. I used to have
"some love for people
"but I have
"no love for Indians

(very softly)
"Dere's
        da baby. Oh,
"sweet little mama

           In Los Angeles
           there was a woman
           looking through a pile of summer
             squash
           for a copy of *Alice in Wonderland*
           the clerk had to come over and
             find it for her
           then she said,
           "oh, this isn't fresh

Tree Talk

Not speaking in human speech
Bearance, bearance
Past forked tongue

The clouds do move

I saw the veins of the face. They
Branched.
The ape is combing his hair
Back, back

The waterfalls are falling waters.
Burns shorter. Flowers nearer
Neighbors make newer.
(Blank)
(Blank) is re-gret, or egret.
(Blank)
(Blank)
Falcon?

(Blank)

But let these different times
Be the result of phrasing
And see how well it is, like limes
Squeezed where lambs are grazing
Are pharmacies

(Blank?)

Brooked back the bucket door, the
Thetis

And Thesis
Combine
Brought up pearls, which
Did shine, ropes (Blank)
(Blank Blank Blank) There was the moon

Tickling,
Trickling down the rear of the eye
Did the trick
That with a hook
Comfort caused
(Change voices)

(Blank)
(Change voices)

Returning you

Ferret, turnips
Which is a matter of reading
They persuade
Rings, turkeys
Which dispersing
Corn, flagrancies
Of a division
Came with feet
Crossed a lintel
Diamonds, rain
College
Of sense
And incense
Diurnal to the toes

Bandy-legged merchants
Of descending
Rings, closets
Rendering
Blood, books (forest?) (Blank) (often?) (off in

Headsets. The criminal
Of durance, with his mammal
Sword, accord, view (With you?)
Past (reoccur?)

Endue.
Imprison.
The feet. The tassel-
dancer (Blank Blank)
(Blank)
(Blank) The beaver (Blank)
Lake Winnebago?
Built?
Out of a hat and some
Corn (Blank)
(Blank)
(Blank)

Lightning-shorn cattle

Impost

They are telling all kinds of stories to each other
In the dark
The pitcher spilt
(Blank?)

From the divorce of a word
From reason
Good sense would tell it
Be quiet
And the coffin comes
Out of a hat and nine
(Blank)

Arithmetic done
By elves and starmen
Look you
You set it right
The Wright Brothers who flew
Over North Carolina and Ohio
Chance song
Dipper
Real line
Home-
ward, the storks
(Blank Blank)
Tree talk

Dream

Jack Hegarty preaching in church,
The Three Hours, his head
looking like a priest's, but in green
high-school sweater, suddenly broke off his
harangue, to point at me and say
"How many shave in your family now,
your father, you, and your cous'?"
Outside,
It was a parish-grey sky, tho 11:40 P.M.
I saw the moon, orangy-yellow, with a piece
breaking off it; then, walking up the hill,
saw the moon again, a ball of orange clumps
of garbage, and next to it, a fleeing
ball of thick liquid or gas, and the sky
was brighter. Knocking on the door,
my brother flung it back like the wind,
and said, "Oh, you've got to see it."
I think he meant it was being televised.

Moon of Green Street

1

Katie sees the moon.

More than one moon. Out there in the South, full moon after full moon
Climbs up into the sky. The moons are like
Fat-breasted hens.

Dizzy men, come out into the light, let us see your
Eyes. The moons are like kettles, lurching across the skies.

Oh, I, the eye doctor, see
Black water and alcohol. A naked swimmer
Lets go of his ankles and dives, down into the mud, at the bottom of your
   eyes.
I peel back the skin of your eye like the rim of a desert. Katie
Catches her breath. The swimmer escapes into nerve, and you
Have the frightened look of a pacifist lab tech.
The delicate operation
Goes on in the bar. Other hands
Lift glasses, other eyes

Wink at the moon.

We are eating thin cactus soup
Out of a clock.

2

Moon of Green Street, I want to see you first. I don't want you
Sneaking up on me, peeping over Lyon Van & Storage,
Giant eyelashes falling like trolley wires.

Moon-laughter makes me sick. Sounds like somebody's
Got a bone caught in his throat. I'm not afraid of you,
Moon.

What if one night, all the bars were closed?
Not even the friendly tap of police feet.
Then, over Buon Gusto, those long white arms,
Over Gino and Carlo's, that obscene leg, that pointed shoe.

No!
The moon's in my dreams, the moon's in the sky.
Thousands of feet up, she sings of her intelligence,
A living, mushroom-colored basketball.

I fear what the moon may know and never say.

3

Kate
         squints at the moon
                              through her fingers
So it appears triple. Three moons
Ride the joints of Katie's fingers.

If Kate were a statue, and with a clink, her fingers fell away,
Where would those three moons be?

4

Will you make me love you and not conceal it?
Though moonlight be foul or fair on Green Street?

The undernourished pygmies of my words
Have tribal shields of hair and paper swords.

And She that bolts her food and scorns her share,
The tasteless Mother of the Faggot Gods,

Crosses our evening in a rocking-chair.
And in her lap, the pumpkin of our words.

The Crazy Bartender

for Gordon Neal

Sorrow reasoned potatoes
Out of nothing. And the muscle of that reason
Are the eyes, ill-formed, unable to see
Even into a riddle. An Irishman meets an Irishman
One night, in the cemetery. "I hears they're let the lepreychauns
Drink," says the one. "Oh," says the other, "lepreychauns?
"Why, there's no sich thing as a lepreychaun, man."

Weepin' an' weepin' . . . Is it children that's been drinkin' my booze?
Children?
My face is white as a ghost's. I run uphill . . . *Who saw my face?*

Then up from the cemetery there rise the teeth
Of old Irishmen I've killed, and there's a stink
That's like the earth itself had too much to drink, and rolled
Over on its side, and said, "Oh oh . . . take me home . . ."
And then the lovely Venus said, "Mars, Jupiter . . .
Fat Green Boy's had it . . ."

I can't sell beer to children. I can't go through those dreams where
Clouds, with screwed-up mouths
Wage windy war on one cell of honey . . .

You'll have to take your chances, bartender.
I bang on the wooden walls of the hotel
The living families laugh, and I'm in hell.

I wake up troubled, wondering why I shaved, and then went right to bed.

The Bad Man

for Bill Whitman

He confuses me, I want to tell you about my insomnia, he
would like that dead horse to get up and run
even if all its skin was canvas. The men
under the horse are sleeping, why don't you?
But it's not a horse, it's a dead horse.
Out here in the desert we don't have time
to be given or to give
soap chocolates. Ha, ha! he screams, what were you
dreaming of, I saw a quiver at the left flank of
what you call canvas.
That was someone I never tried to love.
Tried to? The stars rain. Do you go looking
for the faked-out backs of mountains to prove they don't?
Or do? But I have a whole rock collection.
Legends inspire disgust, legends inspire disgust,
legends inspire disgust. I want my red Indian back
on one knee, like Percy Emerson saw him.

Scared? I said,
you confuse me, confuse me utterly, confuse me
utterbutterly. My knees are water, there's no
place here to hide a goddamned thing.
The horse! Under the horse!
My two dear friends
who nearly made amends
for old and new crimes lie
with space between their ends. And we're out
in wild country, and nowhere near home,
and the rain, and the clouds, crash, and it's all gone
in a minute. The sun

sucks up everything, and smiles.
You confuse *me*, now, said the Bad Man,
You talk like a man who hadn't farted
for fear a territory might be organized around him.
The sense escapes me. Either you're *in*
trouble or you aren't.

My God, man, I whispered, don't you know
the secret of it all? But he stopped me with a finger.
For the horse had got up, the horse had started to caper
with a "Hee-haw" and teeth, the spotted canvas horse,
the high wood hooves. And if that weren't enough
to convince me, he shit. And I said,
"Real horseshit from canvas horses?!"
But the Bad Man was changing mustaches, and said nothing.

The Surf

You listen to the leaves, or watch the leaves
until it is clear,
                    and when walking later
be careful of roads that lead back into yourself

The familiarity of our lives is treacherous.
The familiar   the surf

Ticks in the Rocky Mountains when
I was a kid I thought
would jump off the plants; then
later it was Korea that was dangerous.

Now, to be a person like anyone else
terrifies me.

The Gifts of Death

after Virgil
for Louis Zukofsky

Proteus to Aristaeus:

Your bad luck?
Don't you know the power in it?

                    Unhappy Orpheus
sends you pain, wants you to feel it more,
so mad is he with the loss of her,

who in a game, in a stream, fleeing you,
breathless, barefoot (near death),
ran up on the grassy bank
where slid
                    a deadly snake.

Her girlish kind, and of the trees
inseparable Dryads, cried.
The rocks of Rhodope echoed their lack.
Rings of mourning broke, on
mountainpeaks, men's tongues,
rippling Hebrus, lonely nymphs' lips.

But he, trying to blend his pain into the lute's music,
the pain too new not to have its own words, cried out:
"You, oh my sweet wife, I am here, alone,
by the sea, in the dawn, raw, and I fear the night!"

Like an automaton, he went
to Tainaron, the Ostia of Hell,

a place where leaves shake, though the wind be still,
a Cave, he entered, and came
to a Throne, where the Great Ghosts wait on the King of Shocks.
They unhabited to sympathize with what humans say.
He sang.

A whispering below, a low commotion . . .

•

Thin things, with hints of the human they were,
like pale darts, to hear, alighting
by thousands, like birds
on boughs, in a dark rain
lit by the Evening Star –

They were the rest-
less dead, our wisp-
y mothers, men,
the mighty heroes
lifeless now,
the girls and boys
unsmiling,
the young warrior
in battle killed
by father laid on flames
in filth and blackness kept
where crooked cattails hang
by loveless rippling swamps,
Cocytus, Styx, the names –
Nine times they circle Hell.

And all that Court grew still –
The fiery cracks grew dim –
Like statuary, the grim
Eumenides, crowned with snakes
blue as the mold on bread –
The Dog with Triple Head
agape – and Ixion's wheel
that makes Hell's only breeze
braked, by the poet's voice.

Blasts of air!
and a bright whistling in the Cave.
He is out of Hell, and she
so near (following, as
Queen Proserpina had bid her)
she tastes the light.

When what wild whim of affection
(Certainly, it was a thing to be ignored –
but the Great Ghosts know not how to ignore)
caught him off guard?
Forgetful he,
turns to his Eurydice,
and she sees him, and the Day.

Crash! crash! crash! the words
break. The words of Hell break.

"Who has doomed me, and you, Orpheus?
Who hates so much?"

And then from a little farther away:
"I hear the voices, calling me again.
I go to sleep behind my eyes."

And then as if nearer again:
"Here – take my weak hands!

"Alas, they are not yours.
I am taken away. It is all dark around me."

And as she spoke, she was dispersed
from where he stared,
like when a little smoke
is lost, in blasts of air.

·

Shadows, where she was.

Shadows to reach at
and talk to.

Needing to tremble
in the pain of the thought,

but held, as by hands,
in the pain of the loss,
in a dark so dense
with denial it danced.
What tear? What voice?

Slosh.

Charon guides the raft she goes on, cold.

•

They say, seven months he walked
with the cranes on the streaming banks,
and cried where the sharp rocks jut –
Word after word it came out –

The icy stars

The big cats on the slopes, the soft
breathing, the wind in the oak leaves,

Like the nightingale grieving on the poplar branch
in a stipple of shadows – Was the boy
wrong, that reached in her nest? But her song
is only Where? and its notes are night.

Love cannot curve me.

Do you hear the marriage-
song from the nearby village?

No, I see the glacier.

Snow I see,
not the river.

Frost I walk on,
not the field.

Where?

I ask the gifts of death.

Daughters of Bacchus! Sharp nails
grasp his neck, grip, turn his head.
Enraged, they see the tears.

All his flesh they tear.
It bleeds into the frost.

Ripping Hebrus, Fatherwater,
in your swift midstream you bear the singer's head,
caressing the cold neck. And as you turn it,
once, the pale lips move.
"Ah, Eurydice," it cries, "Ah, lost Eurydice!"

Then right and left, on either side, your banks
echo, "Eurydice," all their seaward length.

Achilles Poem

for Armando

I thought of Achilles,
trying to get at the blood, where it is all
shadow. The life

Odysseus, to whom Death is another place,
like Phaeacia, not letting
too many of them come close at once

trying to get at the blood
The arteries and veins

the jut of the chin and the fire of eyes
beyond the trench,
wanting.

      On the hill, at
11 o'clock, the Searchlight Market closed.
No more ice cream from Swensen's, no more
chilled wine.

Where the "E" car ran, oh
fifteen years ago, when I was a kid,
turned left at Larkin and right again at
Vallejo, to miss the hill. Where Fran lives now.
It seems strange
a streetcar ever ran there,
iron-grey, maroon trim, one door in the middle

I told you all this when I said
it was something else that made me

freeze with terror of the dark,
not the loss
you knew. You said, "Of course."

The hill

tilts me, nightly.

Stars I can see from Union & Leavenworth
high in the sky. They make me think –
It's later than I think. But when I get to Columbus,
they aren't risen yet, they're sunk behind
Telegraph Hill, it's only 12:30.

Cut the throat of the lamb, it flows in the trench. "Baa,"
  lambie-pie.

The streetcar, in an early dream,

a "K" or "L," in the tunnel
turned off suddenly to the left
or right on a new route,
emerged into an underground cavern,
a new world! where it streaked
past lights, and trees – like a model train layout.
This place of dim expectancy
brightened gradually. It wasn't the sun

it was Dawn in the world where I sleep.
But I woke as a child and I wake as a man
to a familiar-ness.
A room.

Oct. 18. 1 want all my love healed.
I want this in! The heartache stilled

(Later) The day. When it seems all these sorts
aren't being played out, sliding downhill.

Oct. 20. I brood over giving, receiving
imagined slights.
Bill says, "Don't call up on the telephone
   and apologize – live with it."
I wonder how these lines will be read

A moth flying around the lamp
that shines through its gray wings

Oct. 21. The full moon rose
with the clearest face I've ever seen.

           I had had all those thoughts about Death,
suffered from them, told them to you
in the bar that night, Love
and my sense of humor
you said were evolutionary. Then grew proud of them
(on the hill, in the other direction – no longer needing
to act out of reasons of power or fame. Love
be my Master (Richard Burton as Antony) Incident
And
woke up again.

                  and the bower-bird
builds,
in Australia,
plants
        stems
in the ground

around a tree
       that keep on growing
and arch, to form his roof.
and a lawn,
tuft by tuft,
       where we look to find something
       when it is no longer lost
As I said, I
           saw the moon

(Later) The days are still,
autumn grey, with heat of breath
A sighing, in and out

Oct. 28. Waking up this morning, I thought
it wouldn't be so bad to die, drowsily,
at the end of life. Last night I saw
ivy, rain-spattered, in the alley outside the Spaghetti Factory,
the big white veins standing out.
Manger says you can tell a man's age
even if his face is smooth as a boy's
by his veins. On the backs of his hands
and wrists.

Nov. 6. We know the body is immortal, but the spirit dies.

Nov. 8. Withdrawing from the feast, Achilles doesn't see
Patroclus crawling out of his little hole.

Robin wrote: "It won't be complete darkness because there
isn't any. One thing will stop and that's this
overweening pride in the peacock flesh."

Ajax stands stock still,
won't answer Odysseus' relentless questioning.

rain on Filbert St., on the steps
leading down into the stars   The

Joy of each thing to be utter,
not frittered away in its connection to other parts

Monday no more than Tuesday,
dying-day, lying-day,
this day in the rain.

      A poem like a hunk of conglomerate.

Can we and it live in this year?
but in the stream-bed, ultimately dislodgeable.
The stream of Time, like one of the freshets on the Sierra,
a trickle in summer, but now, November, with the rains starting,
swelling, foaming over the little dams

Patroclus in Paul's painting
lunges forward, like he does in the sixteenth book of the *Iliad*.

It is existence in reverse, Beauty and Youth
returning, refreshening the Source. It
takes place in absolute quiet, and Hector
and even Apollo seem like cops next to him.

Here in the stream-bed.

Attis

for Harold

This is dying, to cut off a part of yourself
and let it grow.

           The whole self
crawls at the thought of being mutilated,
even self-mutilated, as occurred to me
when you mentioned you had never looked at
the poem about Attis, and neither had I

nor at where in a poem feeling dries up –
A waterfall-filled Sierra canyon dammed
Hetch Hetchy of our spirit. Attis's
cock, in some tree, in some jug of wine
or beautiful lips mouthing Who we love
growing.

So the fireflies go, with small lunchboxes,
mooning around trees. We cut
our conversation off, too, in sacrifice

Birds,
brinks, even
our whole environment, out to the farthest star
you can never reach
(because of light's unchanging speed)
and so your dying can never reach either –

Blood,
not sinking into the ground, mysteriously,
but in the Roman sewers, forever, our home town.

A New Moon

The moon is blank, when new –
A blank board of possibility
I look to the west, or in me – there is no,
not like a sharp note and false note –
signal. It is characterless
and un-
discernible If

What is that to the need for an undenied
change being exerted,
With a sudden sword to cut
notes between us and the stars, Freeing them,
or us, or make a duck walk,
or a watch tick? Cuneyform

or a gravity concealed by
our hands in their usual
ways of beckoning.

You

1

The enemy in the Vietnam war is you. You as I see you; "you" defined by my seeing you. You out in the country, *for example* – and for example necessarily. No one picture – no one *event* of you – relative to other people, waves, stars – no experience of yours, or of you, in, by or with-in life – is you. Nor without my seeing are you, in your sense of yourself, the enemy.

> Oh soft body! Your face
> wreathed in flowers –
> Light and shadow, so, falling

In the village, or between the villages. Not "man," not "humanity." *You.*

Is this over-subtle? Is it splitting hairs to say my country's enemy in Vietnam is not humanity – not the human spirit – but, to put it as clearly as I can, one man *as* he is seen by another?

In the village, or between the villages.

> Where are you?
> I've been looking for you all day.
>
> Ever since eyes have been seeing
> and ears have been hearing,
> listening for news of you,
> wanting to see you. Lips moving,
> words – many, quick words –
> You draw a picture in the air
> to make more clear to me
> what you meant. See?

This is the part that gets in the way of the use that can be made of the Vietnamese. My government does not want to kill people, like the Nazis. My government does not wish to deny political liberty to the Vietnamese people – differences of opinion have their place, in a free enterprise system. Debates, panel shows . . . But we must turn them away from *each other*,

> and bring them
> out of the villages
> and countryside,
> willingly,

> to where the loudspeakers blare
> and the flags wave,

> so that having lost sight of You,
> they will find beauty
> in the *things*
> that pour from the horn of plenty.

2

The Emperor sits across from me.
By his black boots I knew him.

Not right across from me – Look at the picture – he is to
my left (your right). He faces the West.

I crouch
        somewhere in the hills
with a polychrome face,
diseased. I am a Poet. I can't

sit like the Greeks do,
with their heels drawn up against their ass,
their elbows resting on their knees,
rocking on the floor. They counsel moderation in all things.
       How little they know

of the Emperor. He is incapable of excess.

He fingers his dark jaw
thoughtfully. His throne goes down
into the volcano. Beyond Sicily, into the sea.
One of its legs is of coral.

3

I have another story: Our Winking Series of Glowmen.
Your lover died in France. *Red lips are not so red as*
   the stained stones kissed by the English dead.
Now you're a homeowner. You throw a brick at Martin Luther King.
And we've survived the Beatles. They live in a Yellow Submarine.
Mad magazine has survived all that Op Art and Pop Art.
Napalm makes a blister; a keloid. Your whole soft body from the shoulders
   to the waist like a pork skin, the kind you eat with beer.
I have another story: Our Series of Winking Glowmen.

4

Out of all this rubbish – images of sheep, some of them
   lacking clothing,

and the need for sex
                        with my lover
        who is so far away
                        I can't imagine –

The broken handwriting aches itself into scripture.
I try to see again what I have seen –

Why in this broken Empire it is even important
that I write a poem –
                        The railroads
all broken up,
                the spread of
cars,
        The ears that can hear only one word,
        the breath caught in the windpipe –

        Images of sheep, winding down passionate declivities –
        Trees, lifting themselves by their roots out of the land – walking
        so that the whole mass of it shifts – an Arab cloud –

Smoke into heaven –

gasping for breath –

God give me a pen,
make me into a pencil
put in me what I need
and take away
what You want
of me, to tell men
about the United States.

I *am* a man!
Maybe no poet, I guess I've given up rhyme –

I love men – I can't get
A single word out – but I'm rich
in metaphors, but nothing occurs to me
     nowadays,
              but blood, filling blisters
    on the stomach or legs of someone
    that is a friend or lover to someone –

That dinner I ate at the gay restaurant tonight
is thick with blood, Christ's blood.

    Where are you, darling?
    You are God.

    I must not degrade you
    by calling you God,

    Go on away from me,
    be yourself.

5

Sheep come at the end. The world,
suddenly, strangely,
is corpse-still.

But this is what might have been expected – out of the alleys,
and all structures, whether tenanted or disused,

the practical applications following
(on the *hooves* of?) They move faster than we do.
They don't look up, or down.

You will see the red stone
afloat in their eyes –

They don't sniff around your garbage cans, like raccoons.

They are creatures of your own will, you who have learned to dream so well.
The moon hardly moves either, where you sail now, and what was real –

6

The door of gold has shut,
the door of brass has shut,

You sit across from me, Emperor.
Between us a prism.

It is supposed to tell what God will do
with us – it is supposed to appeal –

> There's that special telegraph system
> that goes on between you and Him –
>
> My miscellaneousness must be petty
> to You,
>   Stupor Mundi,
>   I see a lot of sparks

Me–a–spark, he–a–spark, everywhere a spark–spark

Tired of squatting, making up to you –

The door of gold has shut,
the door of brass has shut,

The door of grass, even.

7

No longer do we leave any tracks where we walk,
either in the sand or in the sky above our heads,
count on turned-down cards, lucky
numbers, days,
                 The wind starts again
and the dunes shift.
                   A weed,
with flat green leaves and roots like hair,
you either step on,
                or do not
wherever it is – the meaning of all story
in every step, therefore no story, no rise and fall

except that of the dunes. Nothing will be hidden,
everything will be announced. Take care that you stumble,
that your stumbling does not resemble the stumbling of a man playing at
   stumbling, eyes on the image, some war hero.
       Wind and faces –

Old faces carried down from the highest hills, flushed.
These are the old Sunset sand dunes where I used to walk – prowl,
where all my cruelty has been hidden away.
Man has conquered the "face" of the earth,
drained her eyes. Now all men want "peace and quiet,"
but Memory wants the confluence
undone, the rivers torn away from each other,
one to flow with fire and one with clear water, in which the face can be
    seen, and the pebbles, the flakes of gold.

Feeling Out

1

"Do you exist?" A silly question. "What good is a
newborn baby?" Franklin asked. A silly question, too,
now that we know.

I heard my voice, saying something. I was a newborn baby,
then,
      I wanted to cry. But I heard my voice, instead,
talking a foreign language (English).

Do you hear those voices, trying to be some kind of music?
Do we
      exist? Is it those voices, cries, trying to escape us,
the listeners?

I knew I couldn't go very far, on my bicycle.
Night was a boundary, so was 19th Avenue, but mostly it was my mother, who,
by telling me, became part of me. What was it like for you?

I have to tell you, darling,
I don't take this cheap world.

2

Kinesthesia gives me back the warmth in my cheeks,
the pressure of my lips; the rims of my glasses there
are like part of the air;
                      but I don't feel like I have a face;
I feel like a gate.
            A gate to where?

Words about the darkness get to me; we are ashamed
of our backsides; they are all
phenomenon; we feel to ourselves then
like a fleeing herd.
     I am no cave, I am no
temple, the walls
crawling with gems.
      If you enter me you enter no
darkness (I hope you enter
Paradise (we are so deceived by
sight we can't see this. Do you? I can

keep you out,
with my chin.
I can keep you out
with my mind.

3

Across the Deadly Desert of Reason (What if I
don't let you in, my chin
tilts up, my mind assaults you
like a marquee, is the dark of me
a movie house, are my dreams of touching
fantasy?

(The Baby's body dazzled
before it groaned with logic)

If I open to you I go back and repeat the same
movement again, only slower, my undulant shadow falls
on the Deadly Desert.

Tell me again
what you said, it is possible
everything I think
is wrong.

          No, here,
before we move.

4   The Thaw

The congealedness of my heart and mind
coming apart, coming apart. Angrily striking out, god damn you!
and feeling, knowing, the grasp, yeah, of a god that can damn, that
out of the way!

Poking from inside something, ah, like a cocoon,
poking and softening it with my beak –
a tight and it might have been dangerous nest I made,
my house, ah yes, in need.

And what is inside or outside I don't know. Inside, I was told,
    was sin-side. And outside became pout-side. Well, what
    difference does it make? Those – what are those things?
    Nests, did you call them? I tap them with my stick. The clouds

Yeah, just the clouds.

I was frozen. Well, let's not argue.

It's not just that I wanted it to be a good poem, I wanted to
    be faithful. Well, there was nobody else in that waiting-room.

Martha. The Greek restaurant. Spiro Agnew – well, the fear of
  Spiro Agnew, that exists, persists. And Spiro Agnew wristwatches.
  And the wrong answers to questions. And the silly answers.
  The peculiar way Martha looks at me when. Martha when I.

Sara – Stan – Ping-pong balls with pictures of deer on them.
  The Universe – that old one, too (that lost one?) Then this
  one. Love (Love – I fumble at naming you

Super Bowl. Blood. Death. Unity. I – I –

5 The Ripple

It's all me.

I can say that without any thought of an image of
our separateness or a thought of an imageless   As it all comes back,

it sticks, it becomes
me, like candy.
And I'm alone   I don't know what to do   I turn into myself,
take it all (the world)
and glove it   out of sight   The world remains   a tear,
through which I dying see
the world, relieved of tension
and simple   simple as a leaf.   And it is there and I can step up

into it   and use it again   It is new

Soon it becomes all me again. Then I die again with the pain of
my fingernails, my cock, my toes, my eyes

to still it   It won't go away.   It still remains, its wave,
   its constant ripple, closing in

(I had dinner at the East-West house last night, and met this guy, Tom,
wavy dark hair, mustache, Italian or Jewish I guessed, about my age, I could
see dark chesthair curling at his throat, over his T-shirt. Once he asked me
about poetry. After dinner we got stoned: Knute, Bill Reis, Tom and I. I
asked Knute if he was going to walk to North Beach. Tom answered, said
he was going to walk that way so he could hitchhike to Berkeley off
Broadway. Scared (in the easy chair, me, of unknown he, walking with him,
talking to him. The late empty streets, the dark hills, with – forgot his
name. Sneaked a glance over at him on the couch, dark eyes, mustache –
Who is he? I don't know him. Scared went away, found the Tao again

(As it happened, Knute did walk over. Tom and I and Knute walked down
Bush St., I was in the middle

(From maybe twenty years in the future I looked back on this. Sneaked a
glance at Tom again, walking next to me on Bush St., and realized: I never
knew him. He was a friend of Bill Reis's, used to come over to the East-
West house a lot. I never knew him at all. I *recognized* him

(We walked to North Beach, talking about architecture. When we got to
Broadway & Columbus, Tom said goodnight, and he said to me, "Maybe
next time we can talk about poetry." "O.K." Then Knute and I went to
the bar.

(Twenty years in the future I was sitting on the edge of my bed
in a hotel room in Montreal, examining my hands. There was
late afternoon light. The shade was kind of pushed into the
room by the warm air but didn't move. Looking at the little
moles on my skin   It was all me. There had never been

any other. Had been no one else. Faces, what dreams, I laughed
or remained silent because they
laughed or remained silent. And now not they. Me
on the bed, and it
hanging off there

with no mind of its own

world

6   The Flood
    for Bev

In the night I come to a door, my old house.
On the stairs I can't move. In a dream
nearer to waking I
make myself move, keep
going, don't let it just
be nightmare.

Dragging myself upstairs by the
handrail in the dark and the door
halfway merciless open you
were not there in the dream
but you are in the poem.

A flood of reasons comes down out of nowhere. The light bulb
burned out and why
I didn't replace it and why and why, that accounts for the dark.

A flood
goes by in the air, in the poem, as well as where
the feet wait, so conscious of their toes,
and I wonder
if the metaphors are right, "flesh" for "body," or "swinging light"
for your smile,

and then the flood stops. And I see the
place where it was, dead rock.
And I see the only way across to you is to
step
into that flood
when it is there.

Pleasant Hill

homage to Robin Blaser

Mammy Pleasant's eucalyptus trees,
eucalyptus meaning "well-hidden."
Well-hidden is the need
that calls to my seed.

Outside the dimension in which we walk
notes of another float and are counted
as sweet-smelling leaves.
Her face

appears at the window of the house in the air
that is not there. Questioning
how far style will take you,
how far you can go until it won't take you. The wind

is in the trees.
A single leaf
lies, drying, on my desk, next to the candles,
under the nose of the bear called California, eucalyptus, well-
    hidden.

You turn away from the window.
Is the Universe one fruit
you can get your hands on,
smash through? Can you get your hands on the seeds?

Can you get your hands on the seeds of the Universe,
& fling them to the ground, or fling them to the sky,
& stamp on them there?

There is no inside or outside. There is only
down
into the chicken blood,

and up,
hard as a tree,
hard as my dream of light.

After Verlaine
(Vers pour être calomnié)

for Scott

At 4 A.M. I saw you sleeping
Your naked body in the narrow bed
And I saw – looking for the meaning –
I saw how hopeless all is here on earth.

Life itself is such a fragile process
The mind a flower that is falling apart –
Oh, when I think so I think I am going crazy!
Sleep on, I – Fear keeps me awake, thinking

Passionate sadness to love you – you can do nothing –
You will go breathing then as you breathe now
Oh look closed that death will then set so

Oh mouth, smiling in dreams, next to mine
I hear eternal unloving laughter –
Wake, and tell me there is another life!

Phaedrus

Vancouver–Seattle

When the train went by, eight or ten horses that had been grazing by the railside ran away.

Reading Plato on the train, going past big fields where horses were running. White, fringy manes & hairy tails, dun bodies, not white, off-white, rippling flanks, Eros.

The far landscape moves against the nearer.

The train whistle rips the morning.

The landscape moves like bodies.

The mind keeps its proportions.

Psyche goes with the horses.

Flash, flash, flash, flash. Like that.

Also your old smoke-black snuffly snaggletooth Heehaw Sex, like that. I don't know anything about fucking. I see the horse paths of the gods intersect in the dawn,

where each rides his own.

2

Psyche is mad. It's the Psyche in me that's mad

because Eros has poured flame into me. It was you

I picked out because you resembled the god

(whose name I couldn't quite think of

on the train, going past those fields where horses were running, cattle grazing or sitting, in the grass with their calves. Tiny brown calves could hardly be seen in the high grass. Is this calving time? April? I don't know anything about

generation. I read Plato on the train. Roaring and pouring of his thought. He takes me aloft. I think I will have to worship *your* god, Hermes, because mine, Saturn, isn't one of the Twelve who drive their

horses on high. Saturn never got off the ground.

There is nothing I know about this coming together

gradual moving out of the ego I

enter an image with you

3

Phaedrus. I am Phaedrus. I carry tales
glorifying one old man at the other's expense
& Socrates says, "I know my Phaedrus."

Can I be a lover, who has sucked on criticism so long
& run with strings of talk, like bridles?

4

Eros, Eros, Eros, Eros, winged one
help me out of this tangle.

One glimpse of beauty
past me

holes disfiguring

"you ought not to pursue" – Eros.

"you shouldn't try to steal someone's soul,
    it's a rip-off."

Psyche: "I *am* crazy,
& run off into those deep distances after Eros.
I *am* those horses, Eros." Eros.

5

Big fields where horses run. In the far distance
rubbing against the near distance I can smell
the odours of your body. I don't know anything about
fucking. Nothing of this coming together.

How was it I said it in dream?

I am the boy, I the naked girl.
I stumbled and fell here, imagining you pursuing me;
now I have stopped I see you are not here.

Moving against, moving against, stuff,
tearing, bleeding, my
nakedness surrounded by
bleeding trees. My.

Oh, let me be still.

Unfold from me.

Dublin—Sligo

In the dawn I see the horse paths of the gods.
Men make the day
or slip into th' abyss of thought. In the morning

moving uncertainly, uncertainly, I let
feeling awake, it awakes
between two surfaces

between night and morning,
between lips and skin
and a great brown horse
runs across the field
towards the event
of which we are the moving

& the sunlight on the sheets was like silver flowers

The Words

of a poem are a roundabout way of saying nothing.
The thousand different bird-songs, the thousand flowers
contradict this – they say
Everything is not subsumed (despite Hegel – and Hegel did
    not say this either of course, Hegel is with the
    flowers) the naming
must go on – that is the Way

Tree whose leaves look like a maple,
wild mustard, magenta star.

And here we are. Have we one soul or many?
The sheep, have they
one soul?

Fingers on a keyboard
of sticks and stones.
Some stick and some don't.

Clifden

I wander
in fields alone, crooning

along, over
muddy, spongy ground.

This is what grass is, this is what it's all about –
tough, wide, green strips, degenerate bulbs
without Eros.

Then cinnamon smell
of the hawthorn. Sharp, uncut grass
and the cinnamon smell
of white hawthorn.

Dublin

Is, Is, Is, you said, lagging behind
following the world of discourse
through the choked air
of Dublin.

We can't get free. We can't get through
the obstructions. We cut through
Is and Is-Not, churning the water,
but leaving also the wake. Kindness
where it flattens out and blurs
beyond the explicit. What is it more
I was going to say? I was going to say

Your life is not the arc of thought –
    that peaks lower.
You save me from philosophy
with your Is, Is, Is.

Science Fiction

I was born on this planet.
I will die on this planet.
I walk in the falling rain,
and in moist air after
I carry
a dead bud through an alien sky.

All words become indistinct
when met with an opaque unknown
sticking up out of stuff it was born in
and reliving birth through eyes, hands, words
and stuff which is thrown through the air
as it moves.

All which an enormous image
the size of everything reveals,
then smashes and comes back and pleads
help in a voice like cheese.

I stand in the suck of wind
and splash of rain, and playing cards
fly through the air.

I sleep against the opaque,
traveler, non sequitur.
But sometimes a ghost
breaks through the wall and takes my temperature.

And the rain
beats on the dead bud, the inspecific
haunts its chambers.

I wish I cd write a poem
beginning w/those two lines:

Standing at the corner of 12th & Guelph
Out of my mind with desire

I felt then all kinds of things,
the desire, pain, joy, to be feeling
anything that clear (is this the poem?)

the transparency of praxis, the sweat,
I wanted to love (who am I addressing,
you?

    (your image coming
at me, straight at me, goony –
and then Brian did something, it
was like a sleight of hand, a card
trick (Stop. This is not about Brian.
This is about you. I wanted to love
you then (stop) to (stop) we were newspaper
boys, as we had all been. That was
what it was like then, after the (stop)
our routes, to throw ourselves down on
the grass (I saw you beyond my ideal,
you were not beautiful, you were goony,
I loved you, I wanted to roll around
with (stop) in your arms & smell yr
sweat, unshaven face, all your many
loose, loose-jointed, head tilted,
upward, back, speedster. I was so
happy to feel that, sweating myself,

in the muggy, dull (stop) there
was no sun, I'm not looking for
perfection. I want that relation
(is this the poem?)

that I never got enough of on
the paper routes, I know
it will be this way when we are in
the trenches (women would laugh, my WWII
image, we can't even imagine, I see
myself passing you the gun, we kiss
under a hail of
bullets? stars? The revolution
will have to make room for us,
the revolution in our bodies
will have to
                    (We were doing a route
for the GRAPE, to open up distribution.

My heart is broken permanently.
It works better that way.

The Stick

My father stole my cock from me.
He did it with a look.
He tried to put it back

many, many times.
His eyes almost teared.
He said to me, "There were things
I could have done better."

The night he died,
I said "Good night,"
& he smiled sweetly.
Such little things:

a look, a word, a smile.
And all this while
I have used this stick,
this weapon,
to replace the loss.

Now I know it is not
a sexual organ,
and I lay it down.

Vancouver in April

It's pretty shitty
living in a Protestant city
& my heart too bleak for self-pity

I sit in the Cecil
surrounded by a passel
of loudmouth'd assholes

I swill beer
to still my fear
of the coming year

& there are mornings when I wake up
so riddled with psychic breakup
I can hardly hold on to my coffee cup.

I lived here three months
in a house where I never once
heard anyone say please or thanks.

Not the best indoor weather
for getting your head together
but it's a personal matter.

I walked in the rain when I felt more free
(the rain's great on UIC)
soft Vancouver rain used to console me.

But then I got a job – stripping trucks
for CP Transport. 500 bucks
a month I make, but the job sucks

& the rain gets in my knee
where some cartilage gave way
& I'd rather it were sunny, every day.

I walk to work along Hastings
where every white face seems
skewed by chronic grimacing

& the natives' smashed smiles
pitiful doglike denial
of unadmittable exile.

On Granville Mall trios of thugs
stoned on beer & soft drugs
protrude their blond, bland mugs

(The guys I work with seem all right
In the grimy lunchroom every night
under icetray fluorescent light

we scan the *Province*, don't talk much,
about the fucking foreman bitch
but on personal matters rarely touch.)

Soon will return our German August
& the sullen sons of the upper crust
their bready bodies will loll & toast

At Kits Beach & English Bay
Vancouver resounds through the long hot day
with the intense silence of solitary play

Old men sit with their single glasses
of beer, 'neath murals of buxom lasses
in the vast pub, till the evening passes

after Patrick Kavanagh

Icarus

for Jim Herndon

In the middle of my life I found myself
on a plane from Denver to San Francisco.
Sweaty & shaking from last night's whiskey,
in aerodynamics I was losing my faith.

But the guy in the next seat took time to explain
jet flight, & he blew on a stiff piece of paper
to show how the wing worked, but it fell from his hands,
& I thought, I won't see California again;

we'll crash in the Superstition Mountains instead.
Drank Scotch, sweated more, & prayed to the engines,
while he wrote equations on a yellow pad.

They said: Weightless drop is the price of survival.
Then the plane banked, the Western horizon
steepened, & I passed the crest of the mortal.

Opening Day

for Mike Heintz

They had come back from some explosion, bomb
or quake   in the back of my head   like the beginning
of a splitting

headache, but just the beginning

& then nothing from the other side.

Giacometti hit by a truck, Montaigne
with the stone   rejoiced,

something happened in the real world

but no real world would happen to me
grew more intense   They wanted out

collective

Well, when I had to explode,
I would explode,
and there they would be

my mother's family
Emmett & Frank & Marie
alive & dancing
eating & drinking

I didn't call it a miracle. They were shades
& thru them I could see the smoking ruins
& feel the pain/I have never felt.

(& everybody had their loud opinion
on this   I thought I had to too

thought this real   which kept slipping
back
to the split second
of catastrophe

had to be kept going
by loud opinions

                         •

The Queen's face   face up   in Malone's white box
decorated with shamrocks
                         I danced,
drunkenly, to your Irish Country,
a jar of Guinness in my right hand

splashing/I
fell on my ass, there was

mixed applause.   Mixed with forbearance.

"We pretended we didn't know you,"
you said.   Oh, Mike, I
was pretending

from way back

                         •

But I mistook it. Took the loudness for creation

not cheer. The click
of the pool balls   is more like it   the players
not smiling
unnecessarily.

•

This was a necessary mistake. To pretend it was mine
to make   or speak for   as protected by the prayers

of a hundred nuns/I careened

Larkin St. to North Beach
Potrero Hill to Hamburger Mary's
the Sunset to Haight & Cole

Always in the background were these unsmiling faces
sons   daughters   the girl who sold me ice cream

tender-faced girls, unsmiling
flat, toneless voices.   I ranted & squeaked & cried

Quit yer rhapsodizin', sez Bronley

you are not the first one to be tossed
in the waves

& Bev: You belong

to the City

not the reverse

•

Opening Day at Candlestick
up the escalator

Up the steps to the
sun, & the roar

"travel poster clouds," half of
Candlestick Point sheared off   little trees

terror
           every fist, mouth, mother
and mother-to-be   down the first base line

triumphing

Then the voice came off the crowd:

This Roman mob
grew up out of
La Belle San Francisco
just like I did

& I knew they triumphed

not over me, not over my, mine

mind

not over mind

but over darkness, iso-
lation, as the staring

of windows, the eyes of cars
& streetcars

& most of all the Victorians,
crouched in jealous rows on the hills

tall dark rooms we had stayed in
too long

now out in the sun!

•

Darkness out of which we all had come

& to which we'd go back, if need be.

& back from which we'd come again, if needed.

Mountains and Air

Light Up the World with Your Faith

To build up a world out of strange books,
in the absence of faith. Going to the store
for a pack of cigarettes, going to Prince George,
going to sleep, exactly the same

trip. The hardest step on every journey
is the last, and every step is the last,
downwind from the engine. Yet
   every one of us expecting

(as in a cornfield) realization,
the answer ripening to the question.
To have them both, the breath of hope

in air. After harvest it is impossible
even to lift your feet. The police
shouts in the night, shouts in the brain
   the voice,

tiny but confident, as each grain
is eaten. Answer to answer to answer,
lined up. There is nothing to do with this
but put up with it, live with it. Paper
your walls with it.

27/10/76

Where to get back to the truth
I don't have the truth in my hands

any more. These little stories
don't even need the language,

they use the peril language.
Deep in the middle of everything.
Germany. Your picture of the Saskatchewan
    Wheat Pool.

·

The mist rises
off the river.
The bears come down
to eat the garbage

back of Dog n Suds.
Stand up in the road
like little boys
in bear suits.

This is
Big Rock, this is
Carwash Rock,

early in the season

Lakelse Avenue

No look back
    when you
get out to the edge you see
nothing.

I was born into a world
of appearances, sub-
stantialities, soft
colours, sharp noises,
clouds closing. It
had a rattle.

Nothing has no name
you
  fight to get back
to the familiar
     turns
of phrase, the triang-
ulations of recognition,
the quantum jump

into the next block
under street lights,
ask for a cigarette,

the town shimmers,
trembles.
   Feed this
grinning transparency.

Tell the Truth

Learning to live alone, learning alone
Why? Because there is no other
person yet? No, there may be.
But all seem alike to me, other
than me, not other to me.

To make me up, that was
the way then. Now made up, trimmed
of useless branches,
                foliage hanging
over the road, a good self
but off the road, a limbless
self, good wood, no knots
in me, a pole.

Learning to live alone, learning alone
to live? In Terrace?

I don't know why I'm here unless it is
to be here.   To be *here*.

Oh yes the job that I deserved
like a poker player with a run of bad
luck deserves a flush, & BC Med
is my hole card, which I find contemptible.

My dreams make no sense to me,
    they seem to be
about things I have never heard of
My daydreams too. Someone else
I seem to be, not the old familiar me,

& I'd gladly believe life was a cabaret
or a carnival, or a ship, except that it isn't
This mere state of being is vast

                 •

Glaciers in the arms of trees.
It is a topography, it is
a vast shadow.

Drove up the logging road
3 miles before I realized
it wasn't going anywhere.

Hummingbirds at feeders.
Indian boy, hitchhiking. Bus
trudging through the slush, near Kwinitsa.

Ravens.

From all points
they fly
        to one
heart of being.

                 •

Big fish on the line,
Kispiox River.
Impossible that this
ever be other.

Too many wooden bridges.
Go slow,
take your foot
off the gas.

Each individual
bear, fanged,
each individual
plane.

•

What am I forgetting?

 The fear

that grows from the centre
of a person's being. The fear
of death, the fear of woman

transmuted in the clouds
into a fear of flying,
the engines failing,
the wind's fingers. And yet

the bird escapes the wind's fingers,
soars upward, falls

is caught
by law

by uprushing air

Fewer

cigarettes (marijuana), more
cigarettes (nicotine), more
wine, less beer, more coffee,
less tea, more whiskey, less

swimming, more flying, more snow.
Up there I want to be down,
down here I want to be back

home out of mortality. ("Wouldn't you
want to be their age again?"
sd the lady at my elbow
  before the framed
photos of the graduating class,
early '70s.) What? When? I gave the
expected answer, no, not all that

ignorance, living in an
unreal future again. But this?

Back down to the motel, to get cigarettes,
I heard my boots crunching across the snow,
I saw the women looking at me, it
gladdened them that one so
handsome, breezy, comes in,
gets cigarettes (I dreamed last night

they had extracted the cancer,
a California doctor, charged me
7 bucks & wanted to keep the tissue,

it was dry & spongy in his hand
like dry cod out of a barrel.
I agreed, he could market it
better.

I will come
                to some trivial
point, unable to choose,
the right hand
or the left

                    •

The poem wrestles you
to the ground.

Reg takes the plane up.

I argue
w/Ray Tickson
in Rupert,
that night.

I don't need no
rollercoasters.

I thought we were climbing
100 miles an hour.

n tons of metal,
2 Pratt & Whitneys
hurtling up a

grass blade
vector,
  the seats
next to me filled w/
sleeping women, or
CBC brass, staring
straight ahead

13/1/78

Work Channel,
    & behind it
the peaks, & a loose, orange
streamer of dawn, & the pilot asks us
if we're getting any heat.

The rising air
continually replenishing

Here I feel safe,
even happy, with the water below,
the engines, the radio, etc.
      Why then
does the image of this flight
come back to me

what keeps me awake at night
at the conscious edge, peering
 through vacancy?

I think I can't find my way
back from there, back to the place

I imagine
as

standing at the kitchen counter with
a woman I love cutting
tomatoes & peppers & drinking
a cocktail?

Those mountains
are enormous, every dark stipple
in the snow on their sides
is a tree

•

Hamlet says, this is a place
a point of air & grace
connected with the points
I cannot see to reach,
love unquestioned.

More throbbing, that flower of air
bending to hold us
in the white petals
of the mountains

Up the Portland Canal
sliding on the wind
Pilot looks around as if
he felt someone scared

•

There's only these few
various motions
varied

See all the way
to the coast

Above it
lots of room

(he leans around
holds up his pack
of Number 7

okay
smoke

Slow

You see birds, hundreds of them
in an updraft over Mt. Hays
(or Oldfield, can't ever get
the two of them straight) & you think
of starlings
            clogging the intakes
of a jet at Logan.
                Fear tightened
underground industrial lights & rails.
Winking, moving.

Then you see four birds
against the same hill
one of them overtaking
the others. Look

at beauty, try
to remember, try
to fix yourself
here in nature,
you & it & oh

beautiful word, you,
my father taught me.

"You take those treatments,
& they make you sick,"
he said to me.

It is the loss
I fear, when the cozy cage
of life we build is blown apart by truth

& in the up-
drafts & downdrafts you find your-
self savourless & only an eye

left, darting.

Rupert Winds

Rupert winds blowing
the television set
mind out of its socket.

Not winds of thought, they
are stilled. It is the chaotic
Spring Sunday morning

"the equinoctial storms,"
Marlene Huddlestone calls them.

No particular state of the elements
in itself means more than any other.
Even though Narcissus looked in the water.

The winds of night pour by
disequilibrium & sound
without image.

I feel the look
of the unnamed

& speak the words I have
tenderly:
wind, rain

Chinatown

for Annyha

The culture whirls by us so fast
we can hardly see
things
we called
supernatural

The culture knows
what it knows
& what it calls
the supernatural
is like fried won ton

A Chinese restaurant
Flying knives

through whose doors we push
onto city streets

Hastings & Main & the full moon
light up
the supernatural

•

Sailing above our shadow
with a lighthouse
sticking up out of the harbour
like a sparkplug

when the soul is un-
agitated & the sweet
pneumatic air
lifts you like a pillow

Granduc mine shutdown
announced in New York.
The news transmitted
to Rupert in tones of
reproach.

Out over Chatham Sound I feel the sweat run down my toes.
Am one of those Granduc miners, tied to land & resources.
Person without place an absurdity.

What blather, 70s
poets quote
the CBC news. Pick up

Braudel (easy to read
at this altitude, not like
Martin Robin)

Chinese river transport:
"The richer the merchant
the longer the rafts"

I imagine the Portland
Channel to be the Neva
& Stewart Leningrad
1' above sea level.

Some part of my mind
wanted turbulence, fear, sweat
so it could get the line

"socks soaked" in the poem
Like Bill Cosby says "Neat-O"
or Julia Child on Niçoise
    chickpea pancakes,
"Socca to em!"

Sailing over Tree Point

& peaks of waves

Foam on the channel

Seventh Avenue

for Dick

That winged chariot behind our ears
flashing on the prisms of the air
like the Aurora Borealis, cheers
no one; so we sit each in his chair

contemplating verity. The charioteer
drives his team through our silences
& with flourishes of his spectral spear
punctuates our careful confidences.

We never got a proper curtain for
that window, did we? Broke since January.
Your charioteer is just a character
from literature, an advert for a mortuary.

Quiet your ancient fears, let chains of grace
crisscross the faded dining room like lace.

Paradise Shelter

for Russell FitzGerald – 1932–1978

1

Children's lives
are
fragmentary

They don't know
what's
going on

Episodic,
Robert Duncan
said.

In which rooms
have i seen
paradise

tottered
toward it
& been distracted

in which lives
assaulted
Eden.

Incomprehensible
languages
separate

us,
we grapple
w/fragments

of reason
shattered
mind.

2

Did vacant lots
and bare squares,
bourgeois parks

breathe back our words?
All irregular
perspectives

beckoned
(mouthwateringly)
& took the heat off us

& we strolled
becomingly for our time
imparting the requisite

quantum of gladness,
a feather
in the balance.

3

Did some now-hidden
goddess nurse
our freshly shaved
philosophy?

Wit fueled by anguish
& contempt
but flowering into
story yet

Thought public as all Hell
but Art,
the way (Der Weg –
Olson) lost

The method hidden
from ourselves
Hermetic
not by choice

1961,
New York.
Paradise
a joke.

Where Hell is
people live
Your eyes and mine
decided that

& then later in Hell
swallowed the New
like a corrosive chemical
Stupid to blame culture . . .

4

In desolate
location
innumerable

projection–beam
universes
flash

Who dare dream
of happiness
They don't know

what's going on
what dreams
underlie

every step
even those
that stumble

The dreams of the blind
the numb dreams
of the one

whose worship
has been found
wanting.

5

The Emerald City
shining over
the burnt-out slums
of North Philadelphia.

Like reality,
the approaching
PTC streetcar also wobbles
on its tracks . . .

A splendid mockery
or a mocking splendour
The altarpieces you fashioned,
Michelangelo-like, in your mind

the world that while it loved you
gave its dreamlike substance
to be modeled
by your vision

& the lapsed, gutted churches
where even
the name
cannot be found.

6

& the body
which we all are
(like M.
came by to tell me

the goats
cd be sitting in our chairs
& us outside
trying to make a meal out of dandelions

7

You perhaps
of all of us
did not desire
to dominate.

Armando said,
he asked me up
to his room
to draw me
    & he drew me!

Eyes
at rest
the pencil
moving,

no "privileged observer"
in that world,

this world,
or quest

imagined
unshackled
unselfish
love.

Did not
"condescend"
to illustration,
  no auteur he,
    "separate reality"

monger, or hiero-
phant.

A gawky
28-year-old Pennsylvanian.
Antagonist
of the game.

"They're furious
that a six-foot Irishman
like me is queer.
You, they expect it of."

                •

Heroes
in your life,
men

pursued by demons,
                    Spicer

named you Billy.
It was a ring of words
It rang through all the places
outside the words.

                    •

The dark face
found its crown
(The body grew fatter.)
The steady look became

a long, limp gaze
on man
& woman.

Parsifal, Percival.

8

Whatever this place is
that we will not admit
to each other we have discovered
is all there is.

Each unapproachable and fiery self
physically and symbolically
involutional.
Hiya Buddy

sighted across blocks,
universes passed us
like streetcars.
We clamber

on the
outside – parasites,
we can't make contact
through our life-support systems.

A birthday candle,
a light, a shadow
or something you saw
in the air around you,

a being seeing back.

Wordless acquaintance
in search of procedure
each act of
paradise shelter.

Teenage Boredom Poem

It is difficult to hide the despair
when you look at the children
The teenagers confront a void
they call boredom, i thought what they
faced was a structured continuum

A gap between standardized items
readily identified as hot dog,
breast, car, the question they
ask then, am i normal, is my
reaction to girls' bodies pure
of any personal, is it all done
to me, do i cue in?

(If the number of items
held up for attention
is gradually decreased
(for more predictable
marketing of) do the items
expand to fill up
the mental field, or are there
gaps (connective tissue?

The teenagers have seen
the connective tissue, the wiring
in back of everything,
through the gaps between the receding
commodity universes,
               they sense,
as if it seared their hearts, the world
(that, early, seemed to tremble
at its inward-folding edges

w/mystery & promise), is
destroyed, denatured,
intimately torn,
                what's left is
components, death masked as
life, backlit, to buy

Difficult to hide your despair
seeing what teenage eyes (so few)
glimpse between the blocks
of commodities expanding to fill
the only dimension of the mental
field, eyes
            dart, see
no RCMP, pursue
wisps of thought,
images (forgotten beauty, go
back to geometry, leaves,
snowflakes, beauty was known
then (now queer), but minds
give out, give in, too few,
call it boredom, bow heads
humbly to what is, idea
of the world deadly, off limits,
queer, be like everybody,

then look at children,
younger, clear, inquiring eyes,
cosmic wit, peak of evolution,
an infusion of the divine, no matter –
by then the grid
               will be complete,
they will be turned into relays,

buy hot dog, see girl's breast,
react, quick, buy soft drink,
memory burns
for a year or two, unutterable
longing & loneliness, then moon,
stars, too, are commodities.

The Hangover

for David Phillips

There will be more hangovers
The days that danced once
are prisoners, of the years

The seasons shock us
w/unbidden power, & we drink
when it thunders;
when the land that spins in the stars
speaks
flower & shower
we feel spoken too & drink

& shiver w/the thrill
of the immortal gift
of recurrence as present
enjoyment, as act

but even on long spring evenings,
darkness gathers,
the day, obedient to the year,
her lips sewn shut & the number off the calendar
pasted on her forehead, steals past

We drink to defy that vision
Time sucks at the insides of our heads,
dries out
our voices

There will be more hangovers
Lonely mortality will walk Quebec St. again

sick of the horror, of the non-being
of love in us (as in a childhood dream
thumbs & arms & ordinary nearby objects
swelled & loomed, ominously, so the soundless
    presence

of human screams, the clench
of entropy
muffles & deadens the soul

Each one knows his fate on the hangover
not unique, but to be suffered uniquely
It seems unbelievable, fatuous, that we might return
from within the word, from within the flower
The head is concrete, the air waste,
the whole is figured, mockingly,
in the knowledge we seek to escape

& escape

Pub Night

    This i record
that listening to you talk, my mind half on you
& half on the variousness of what you were saying
    it struck me
that love is true, not just real, not just a
    sentiment.

I was afraid i might forget this, so i grabbed
    a cigarette pack that was lying on the table,
tore off the top, & wrote:
    "Truth has a double
    value: obverse/reverse"

(A couple of days later i find it
    in my pocket
& i tape it in my writing book, under this
    quotation from Duncan:
    "I never made any vow to poetry
    except to cut its throat, if i could
    make somebody laugh."

(The tab of the cigarette pack has an obverse too,

it says:	Player's	FILTRE	
	You can't beat	Rien ne surpasse	
	the taste of	le gout des	
	Player's	Player's	

& by "obverse/reverse" i mean
one Truth, i hope, not two,
not a scattered, shattered love
falling through endless darkness
but a mystery, plain & simple

as a glass of beer (& needing many
of same to perceive, no doubt, but
when perceived, perceived with a
lessening of tension, as something
simpler
           than terror

A Patriot's History of Oz

for Jess

The Wizard of Oz wants to go home.
He huffed & he puffed & he blew his house down.
Dorothy & the other vagabonds whom she has attracted to her train
arrive in Paris.

Coup d'état foiled: General Jinjur's
Amazons driven back at the gates.
Scarecrow Claudius & the enlightened
Tin Woodman playing Jefferson to the Winkies.

From the North comes the changeling & the animals are banned.
A bourgeoisie rises on the powder of life,
Ozma's magic
mirror, & Glinda's book.

Wispy borderland queens
(wanting a part) hasten
to deliver the family arcana
into the capable, hairy hands of Professor Wogglebug.

But some districts in the Munchkin mountains
are still not recommended
for the itinerary of Aunt Em
& Uncle Whatsisname.

Gentle Northern Summer

1

Looking out window at neighbour's spread,
vast spaces "bourgies" think they deserve . . .

(Why judge? What do I care?)

Later, on the grass:

Gentle northern summer, do I face
my uncaringness when my mind
is filled with you? In this gentle time
of trees & bees & clover feel a wordless
reprobation to discover

behind their placid faces & doors
a secret that unites them, willy-nilly,
with the coal trains coming, five years
"down the road"?

(coal dust on leaf & air, in
nostril & ear, 500-mile-long smudge)

(A mile from the tracks you don't
notice the whistle, in the buzz & hum
of insects & reliable appliances

(Nor 4,000 miles east do New York bankers
coming out the glass doors of their Park Avenue
ziggurats see any coal dust either
in the edited texture of events their eyes
pick up

(30 km south my neighbour, F's, pickup
crosses the red cantilever bridge
over the Kitimat River & speeds up the hill
& as he makes the turn at the top, he takes in
the view, of the Kitimat Valley, mountains & mist,
    splendid –
takes it home with him, in fact, it's part of his
lifestyle
            but the clearcuts that hang over us
(like swaths made by the teeth of aliens)
are not part of the "views" we appropriate,
they are external
                    the scraped
slopes evidence value
racked up somewhere, some
big account
            Haul it out,
& then we'll go mining. And the ranch houses
stay put, tame trees on the lawn,
on the crimeless streets

2

for Daniel

At a table in the old Houston hotel:

"Each time," Vivian said,
"people got moved out of the way,
Indians, then farmers, then came the mill
& mine, & now" (swinging her arm wildly) "that mall,
that none of them know what's happening to them."

("The real Trojan horse," Spicer wrote,
"was Greek sentence structure. The Trojans
never knew what hit them.")

*People of this north will have to change
their ways* (some newspaper)

      Who counts
the changes? a child growing up
in Houston, say, to Indians, bear & moose

(swimming across the river to the hippie houses
& their eyes told / what had moved them)

to teenage void & foreseeing heavy industry
knocking the moly out of the mountains
(not Homer's herb / that kept men sane,
protected from being turned to pigs,
but silver grit that hardens steel for war
to see who will control these malls, these stalls

He sees the bland & bowed consumer heads
in Ali Baba's cave, pass the tumbled piles
of glittery cloth, cold sparkle of death games,
pink Mexican fruit,
their eyes all inward turned
on private catalogues

At the checkout stand he sees
the illusion & the cash
change hands (with thank you on both sides).
The former goes eventually to the dump

(of things that cease to charm),
the cash goes to Vancouver
(by computer),
                    & sees, *we* are the natural
resources, that "mix our hands with the earth"
& drive from mill to mall to spend our pay –
the suckers at the breast of dreams

If all this were brought down
quite suddenly, he'd say
people'd rise up in anger
(but with no world to compare it to?)

(& it done slickly, equipment
moved on site, oiled, the go-ahead
archival by the time the wheels turn)

(& if they dare,
the system, the tangled boundary
(that has no place in what we learn as place)
deflates, at every encountered point
draws back with a gasp at being
unappreciated, dangles some plastic
goodies in our faces, some go-cart

& we go off gaily in the snow
follow the moose droppings

then it swells up again, aggrieved
but deferent, gets to work, pumping

value

3

Looking out the window I can see
nothing of the life I'm buried in,
slippage, moraine –

The ranch houses
like a row of broken columns,
tame trees on the lawn. Behind them,
the half-wild second growth in their hundreds,
hemmed in by the bench. More houses,
in the air, some for sale.
It is so still & dreamlike.

To get one more tankful of gas,
I drive to the pump.
Like my neighbour, I accede
to the coal trains coming,
the rearming of Japan, whatever.

The secret is not in the picture.
It is in some closeup of our lives
that we cannot see, smeared over us
like a recurring decimal.

San Francisco's Gone

for Gerald, much love

and in memory
of Edward Dermott "Ned" Doyle
who taught me poetry
and gave me reasons to travel
north of California St.

1

For a fraction of a second behind tired eyes
image of SF waterfront circa 1950
from deck of SP ferry
                            emerging from beneath
double-deck Bay Bridge; splayed piers flank
Arthur Paige Brown's Ferry Building,
'20s skyscrapers, Russ & the phone company,
& the nozzle atop Telegraph Hill, in scale
with the human houses, high-ceilinged neighbourhoods,
ascending steep slopes of bluebrown Twin Peaks.

All night drinking on the train
from Stockton: USF football game,
Dons beat COP 56-7 (?)
   – the train must have been shunted over Western Pacific tracks – I think
   we passed through Tracy – or held on sidings, to take all night to get
   from Stockton to Oakland (80 miles?)

I started drinking beer that summer, with Tom Gallagher, Bert Schaefer,
   and Neil Battaglia, in Tom's car, parked somewhere out in the Sunset with
   the lights out, a weekday night, cold quarts of Burgie or Regal Pale in
   paper bags

In June I'd graduated from SI, walked up the centre aisle of St. Ignatius twice – once for the Martin Latin medal and once for the scholarship to USF – then last, in alphabetical order, to accept the ribbon-tied scroll from the priest sitting in a carved armchair below the altar (my rival, LaForest "Frosty" Phillips, beat me though; he went up for three prizes)

I was a sissy in high school, & got picked on a lot, & so, started hanging out with these older guys, Tom, Bert, and Neil (whom I'd impressed with my wits, I could make them laugh), I'd met working as a page after school at the Main Library (McAllister & Larkin, architect George Kelham, 1917 (?)) & drinking beer (so maybe it was earlier than that summer)

Drank vodka (in a bag) for the first time at a college "smoker" & woke up the next morning in the back seat of somebody's convertible, splattered with the necessary dried vomit, the car being parked not on any street but askew in the parking lot at the centre of campus, many students at 10 o'clock class break peeking in the window

& became a football fan. That year the Dons went undefeated, so, traveled on the chartered fans' train to Stockton to see them whomp COP. Next Monday USF was ranked 10th in the UPI coaches' poll. 1951, Ollie Matson's year.

San Francisco, as it looked then.

2

Her first day at the office
all lunch hour she walked round the block
too shy to go in a restaurant

One of several times I visited my Aunt Catherine, my mother's younger
sister, a nun in her seventies, at the convent in San Jose, she told this
story. We were sitting in the sunny visitors' parlour, on spotless
upholstered furniture, that had been my mother's.

If she went to work at 17, that would have been 1921 or 2. I imagine the
building as Kelham's Standard Oil of California headquarters at Bush &
Sansome (that went up in '21). After her dad lost his coal & wood yard
in Daly City (gas now cheap enough for cooking), she had to go to
work. Big corporations were hiring women for office work – SP,
Standard Oil, PG&E (that sold the gas). Catherine would have been 13.

California corporations put up neo-Gothic skyscrapers (25 storeys, tops) on
landfill placed in the '70s over the wrecks of sailing ships (the original
waterfront was just east of Montgomery)

I imagine the block she walked around as Bush Montgomery Pine
Sansome, every building new or under construction, bare steel & the
flash & sputter of oxy-welding, excavations, wagons, horses, men: a boom
built on fire-insurance proceeds (five Eastern companies bankrupted) &
loans from the new Bank of America (backed by grain & fruit receipts)

Jack had come out from Cork in the '90s. (His cousins in Menlo Park
who had emigrated earlier thought of Jack (and Mamie, whose father
Michael was a day labourer) as "Irish," but considered themselves
"Californians" (this is also Catherine's memory).) When he lost his
business he went to work for C&H Sugar, the Hawaiian growers' refinery
in Crockett. Boarded, came home weekends & Christmas. The gold 25-
year pin with diamond chip, which he received on retirement (and
which was sent to me after Catherine's death, in 1985, by the Sisters),
reads: *J. Hennessy 4–16–41.*

25 years a farm boy in Cork, 25 or so an Irish-Californian worker, then
merchant, then at 50 a sugar worker. Mamie and the four children
moved back downtown, to a flat in an alley off 15th & Church. Marie
would have taken the J, or one of the Market cars, to work. Mamie (or
Mary, as she wrote on job applications) went to work for the SP, when
Catherine and Francis were older.

For it was Mary, Mary
long before the fashion came

Marie, a French name, why? A cachet
of elegance, before the Fire?

Though with propriety, society
would say Ma-rie

And the shyness, of the Catholic girl,
near country girl, grew up on a kind of farm
next to a coal & wood yard

Brown hair, fair skin, freckled.
Hazel eyes. *Petite*, five-one.

Learned her Palmer hand
at Mission Dolores, typing
at the office. Early as I can remember,

the grocery list with one or two items
neatly crossed out. She could balance her chequebook.

3

The first-born, her brother Emmett,
graduate of Sacred Heart, attending
night law school at St. Ignatius, working days
on the front desk at the St. Francis: their hope.

Imagine a weekend excursion to Santa Cruz.
The SP train leaves from 3rd & Townsend.
Emmett, his sister Marie, his girl friend Regina,
his friend George Stanley from the hotel.
Cousin Mary gets on at Menlo. They take

a couple of cabins in a tourist court
near the beach. Do they bring
blankets from the City or borrow the ones in the cabin
to spread on the sand? The striped
beach umbrella goes up, the girls in one-piece
suits (& caps if they go in), the men
in baggy trunks run in the surf, their feet
slap the wet sand, they bat
the beach ball. Big green waves
off Monterey Bay break.

In the evening
they walk the boardwalk, or "invest"
a dime in the player piano with seven
percussion instruments banging in the Casino.
Throw the baseball, knock over the milk bottles.
The booth lights glance in the soft waves
of the girls' hair.

& back at the cabin play swing records
on the wind-up Victrola (I guess),
& later in the decade
mix orange blossoms: canned juice
& bathtub gin. Young, happy
white-collar workers

Happy to return to the City

4

George (there was a photograph, part of his face
   in slanting shadow, the mouth obscure)
was in the Navy,

was out in the Atlantic once, on a destroyer but
   not far, nowhere near the U-boats
(the war – for improvement – like the Panama Canal)

At Pelham Bay Naval Station, New York, he had 'flu.
Discharged in '19, sailed for home, & to return

to his widowed father, George Albert Stanley, civil
   engineer
and Grand Secretary of the Young Men's Institute (the
   Catholic Y), club & baths at 50 Oak St.

living in an apartment on Turk, or Octavia . . . check the
   city directory.

The ex-sailor was George *Anthony* Stanley,
the friar patron of lost belongings exchanged
for the Prince Consort. And that was his mother,
Molly McCormick's, gift.

Did Marie tell me he wrote poetry? Or that, en route,
   he stayed, several days, a sojourn
(or was it just a shore visit, a few hours?)
in Havana, Cuba, & thought of not
coming back, but going on to Brazil?

because that's where I imagine him, a serious –
   a dreamy, dark, narrow-headed boy,
      with stiff black hair. I see him at a table (marble top)
      in a sidewalk cafe, or walking the Malecón
      into a summer wind, but can't imagine how he imagined

that break, what image, song, or deeper will
called him –
                    but instead returned

to the Grand Secretary, who lives at the William Taylor
   Hotel on McAllister, & takes all his meals out now,
      accompanied by his boy,

and a job on the front desk at the St. Francis.

Emmett invites him up to his mother's place, at 11 Carl.
In the front room Ma plays the upright, a
vigorous bass, bright treble, plinking
above high C, rippling streams.

Then the girls gather round chorusing,
"Come, Josephine, In My Flying Machine"

& the men, in good clothes, seated
on Mamie's mahogany furniture, served
cake & claret.

5

They were good houses, built by small contractors working out of sheds in
    alleys, mixing concrete & pouring foundations, blueprints on site. On the
    side streets –
Clayton, Shrader – wider types of Queen Anne Victorian – big, gabled
    attics, broad sidewalks for play. On Carl
(the arterial, later the car-line) older, narrower styles,
    flat roofs. The Haight
is forty years or so old, in '33. Sunny Jim had been Mayor,
now Governor. You repainted your house every five years, you & your
    brother-in-law. Borrow the ladder. With a hoist you could tar your
    own roof.

Now down the north side of Haight of a Spring morning comes Mrs.
    Murphy, a fat (not stout) French (Franco-American?) lady, in black (like
    the other morning shoppers) – black straw hat, black purse, & in the
    purse the worn leather change purse; from the Superba, crossing at Cole,
    in front of the stopped Haight cars, wagons & trucks, to Romey's, to get
    cantaloupe or celery 3¢ cheaper. Her new downstairs tenant, Marie
    Stanley, often accompanies her, but not today, she ran up Carl to her
    mother's place, number 11.

The front parlour of Ma's upstairs flat (Marie walks down the hall) is silent,
   as is the back dining room. Jack is in Crockett. Marie sits at the kitchen
   table. Ma comes up the back stairs with marigolds, picked from
   slat-bordered beds in the backyard. Pokes the fire in the grate, moves
   some stewing apples away from the heat, pours coffee. She sits down
   across from Marie, who tells her hesitant secrets.

Sunlight sparkles in the high windows; outside, clothes on the line wave,
   trees in other yards. The bride & the bride's mother talk, of the new
   husband and the old one, the one away, the father. The things to be done
   for the men who come home.

(When I saw the bride's face at Carew & English
not looking upward from the satin,
I saw by the line of her jaw it was my grandmother's,
previously concealed by amiable laughter)

6

& George went to the PG&E for a year –
on the metal monster, through the new Sunset Tunnel –

then the Hall, with its green-patina'd dome
   (was it gilt in '15?), Arthur Brown, Jr.'s
couchant sphinx-headquarters, with wings for legs
   (when whizbangs flew & mustard gas crept
at Ypres), colonnaded tribute to Sunny Jim Rolph's
   honest administration, and symbol
of the new City risen from the ashes, after

years of graft, trials of the Board of Supervisors,
Boss Ruef's creatures, interrupted by the Fire,
    was to be
the major effect in Daniel Burnham's "City Beautiful"
    plan, if hungry businessmen had not
sunk that dream (hardly vision), gone back to
    making money on the
old plat, stacking the bricks the morning after
the Fire
            (and well they did, can you imagine the City's hills
draped in landscaped avenues, like ramps on the contours?)

    The Fire that George remembers (he was eight,
walked with his father to the north/south ridge of the City,
    Laurel Hill cemetery (they were living somewhere out
on Turk), walked with thousands up to the Park, there
    they turned around, looked east.
On that April day, winds blew. Sky was red. 50,000 people
    stood & watched
the red sky, & then the red & black sky, & heard
    all day & all night, the roar
of the flames, & the falling of buildings.

& on the weekend, smart guys neatly stacked the bricks
(but who could, Bean says somewhere, tell the lessees
    from the looters?)

7

Late afternoon. Fog comes, in gusts, streamers,
then a damp wall over the Park. The custard-white
spires of St. Ignatius shine bright above. Like bishops.

Sand is still blowing in the Sunset, houses
hammered in the sand dunes, boys climbing in the unbuilt.

8   Under the Dome

A 12' oak-paneled office, upper walls off-white.
Black tabulating & card-sorting machines. The boy sits
at an unused desk, randomly fingering the keys
of a comptometer. The man turns

from the women in black smocks with white
lace collars (who turn too), a white card
in a black wood frame, held out,
a word in black caps, glassed:

> ## THINK
> IBM

Then down the marble corridor
of the north wing to a second office.
Women looked up from their typing,
they worked for him, as he worked
for Mr. Brooks, & Tom Brooks worked for Mayor Rossi.
   Part of the dome is seen,
chalk-green, in a window above him.

FDR was President, Pius XII Pope, Joe Louis
heavyweight champion. We were winning the war,
a sure thing, but he, though complacent

as any Democrat, disliked the routine.
He knew the City was built on sand and an
underground river, that they pumped
water out of the Opera House basement
　　24 hrs. a day.

What was in front of
my face when he held out
that card in its black frame
but his body, white shirt, Paisley tie
hanging, belt & buckle. (The card lay
in the top drawer of the highboy years,
　　under socks.)

When he threw me in the ocean
I can't even remember yelling,
only running back up the sand
to the umbrella, remains of picnic lunch.
Ocean Beach. (The sand was dirtier now,
there were things in it. Bottle caps.)

In his office he tried to show the boy
the trustworthiness of the City, souls
shaped by official duties.
He couldn't believe it.
So we went back to water.

In the clammy indoor pool
of the YMI, the boy
willed his body to sink, would not
be buoyant.

Of what
importance is it except to do
justice to the pain of his want,
his lack, holding out a gift that was not
his to give, his version of manhood, boyhood.
He was not a giver. He was a poet,
    a sailor,

manqué. The boy rejected
the mirage projected
from some beyond
& bounced off Ireland.

We stood naked in the shower room
& his will backfired on his eye,
his secret passion stole the boy away
on waves of adventure, & in that moment,
    his lostness
was the true gift.

9

Once, on the streetcar, the "L," going downtown,
a sunny Saturday, maybe the fall of '47,
him 48, me 13, heads bent, an intense
conversation, in the dark, varnished seats
at the back of the car. It had begun

even before we sat down, taking transfers
from the conductor (were we going
to the ball game?) I could tell

he wanted out, that he looked towards San Diego
(we had spent a couple of weeks there, that summer)

as he had to Brazil. There were breezes & shadows,
the metal monster rolled smoothly along Market
from Castro to Sanchez. He had a grey hat on
with the snap brim turned up
all around. We wore thin McGregor jackets,
grey or beige. We were almost friends.

He told me what it meant to be
George Stanley, with only wit as a plea.
He tried to pass on to me
the name, Anthony, his mother had found
to replace the alien Albert. He wanted me

to be Tony, it fit the land, he said, like Mission
architecture, women liked it. I could not
take that talisman, happiness, from him.
Loyally I chose to continue his fuckup.

10

Ten years later he comes home on the L,
the pink *Call-Bulletin* folded under his arm,
takes off his hat, in the kitchen
lifts his glass of Roma port to her, tells her
(again) how he hates the place,
the Hall. The leisurely civil service manner
adopted by Blacks or Samoans seems to him
misconduct.

11 Islands

All the islands swam across the Atlantic
and became parishes in New York.
– James Liddy

But James, some of them must have swum
further, by Panama portage come to a Golden Gate,
a Catholic country whose cathedral debt was paid
by transcontinental train time ('69).

Shanty Irish
south o' the slot, & lace-curtain Irish
sticking flowers in vases to place on tables
even when there was nobody dead.

Tobins
of the Hibernia sucked deposits to the
heights (like, Ashbury?), & lent them out
past the panic of '73 when even Ralston
(of the Bank of California, he who had planted
eucalyptus seeds in the Panhandle) jumped in the Bay;

small factories, one- or two-storey buildings,
iron workers, brass founders, flour millers,
stitching bags to fill, wagons to carry
   cross town,
living in flats over stores, yet building,
out Mission & Howard & Folsom (where Mission makes
the big bend towards Spain), *palaces* . . .

"copies of fragments of palaces . . . thin, wooden, box-like structures with
   bay windows," thus Arthur Paige Brown's scorn for the people's

mansions, Victorians he saw first in the '80s,
brown-wallpapered, tintype-laden, gas-lit,
that packed the 11th ward, & pushed out

towards Daly City, farms.

Small families. Not because of safes
but diphtheria. To their priceless
children, nuns spoke
blandly of Hell, at the bottom of space,
with its tortures,
                              & even in the public
schools, teachers said, "absolution,"
faced down nativist rage.

The islands: St. Joseph's, St. Rose's, St. Peter's.
St. John the Baptist, on Eddy. St. Agnes
(of the Haight). St. Anne of the Sunset.

12 The White Cliffs of Doelger

Henry J., developer, when land was free
& work was cheap (& the 17 car 5 cents)
financed and oversaw the building of
good houses in long, north–south blocks

on the Parkside slope. Retained damp sand
by concrete wall, water pipes
the City put in, big creosoted redwood poles,
crossarm'd, upheld the wires (as they still do).

Each bungalow, stucco'd, painted white (a few
pink, yellow, green – the colours of frosted cakes)
looked down blacktop streets with white lines

to the Pacific. And the ocean breathed its condensation back
high as Twin Peaks over my head
all spring & early summer, morning's womb.

13

From the earliest she dwelt in Heaven, its brown, sloping hills,
that California bruited as an afterlife
for suffering Ireland. Gossoons,
unmarried at 40, made their way here,
stepped stiffly from the train at Oakland Pier,
bachelor uncles needing to be cooked for.

These were the duties of the daughter, to turn
the profusion of Paradise into family meals.
The gas range saved her labour but demanded
by its white enamel hauteur more devotion
(& kneeling polishing Mondrian linoleum)
than her mother's wood floors & coal hod
& lump coal in dusty bags leaning by the pantry.

Then needed a green car to drive her mother
to doctors. The young men of the good time still wearing
collar & tie toed it to the Park from the rest home run by
"that woman" to whom she wrote cheques.

She was on *some other work*, her clothing,
serviceable coats, hats with perfunctory veil,
showed it: determination & later hair colour.
She wore flowers like they were ornaments.

In the bath she would wash my hair, then rub it dry,
brisk, detached. The phone would ring during dinner.

And kept all the accounts. Angel of mercy
arriving on time, Hayward or Hayes St.
   Later schoolchildren
knew her reliability, her love.

In the hospital, on Darvon, she patted her thigh
where the cancer grew & said, "My friend."

14

After her death, George & George & Gerald
walking up Taraval from the Riviera Restaurant
(not North Beach of the '50s, but credible Italian food,
water & a basket of bread on the table before ordering),

Dad walked away into the shade of a building
to pee. So there we were, like we didn't need
facilities. No longer separate in time, but in fact
friends, boys, three sons of a dead saint.

15 Her Dream

In the Sunset, in the '50s, her soul breathes easy.
She walks to the retail, noting with approval
disappearance of vacant lots, sand & iceplant,
houses & stores going up, even without lawns,
flush with the sidewalk; & from her back window sees
terraced houses, white blocks,
covering up the dunes, leaving only
a strip of beach: families moving
in, taming finally this almost empty
Spanish shore, home to seagulls, a sense
of reward for rightness.

      Now there's happiness,
a living room furnished from the Emporium,
rose brocade drapes, gold sofa & chairs,
tables, & friends make up a club, a parish
salary-rich, a new church, bell
tower & baldacchino (fixed canopy over the altar)
rises from the striped parking lot
(Archbishop Mitty charged the going rate on the loan).

The City is built now, it stays poised
here for a moment, respectable,
inviting speculation, till a generation
dies or moves down the Peninsula.

Marie has the club over
after Christmas midnight mass.

A police lieutenant, the vice-president
of Cal-Pak, big men in blue suits,
gripping highballs, stand in her living room
(& George stands among them, in white shirt & tie, but not quite
of them, something odd about him, McGinty, the VP, has said,
not unkindly, mind somewhere else.

                                 Marie bustles
among the men & their wives, with hors d'oeuvres.
The blue & silver balls gleam on the artificial tree
& Crosby sings on the hi-fi, "Adeste . . ."

After they leave something takes her back.
A holy card in her missal. Her thoughts go back
to the Mission, she sees again
the crowded streets, where it all went on
in flesh and blood. Streetcars clanged,
priests hurried past, to the sick,
her aunts dressed in black for shopping,
butcher on 16th St. with the sawdust
& pink butcher paper – living world –
& all seemed to know it was one –
bread meat fur flowers –
moves her heart, not Paradise
but plain reality lost.

Illusion, I want to tell her.
Like the Milky Way, the galaxy seen
through its longest dimension, packed with stars.

I want to tell her the stars walk alone.

Time packs truths closer, events flock on
   hills of knowledge
(& she nods & smiles, dreaming alone)

Her truth now wakes in my mind
& where there was bleakness or a gash in meaning

(George & George & Gerald sat in the coffee shop
on Polk St., a block down from the hospital,
commenting lamely on the service, the waitress, even
halfheartedly joking, for each other, then in silence
turned back to her again, her worn, sweet face – she
loved – it doesn't matter who

We can part, Marie & I,
if we can each remember
a mother whose eyes showed care,
the home look

Sometimes, a heart waits
unable to answer, or do more than
look from the window,
fondly, unseen

Marie, who bore me.

San Jose Poem

for Catherine Hennessy
(Sister Maureen) (1908–1985)

Starting in April, sadness
carried forward from Catherine's death
which I have not mourned, in April,
in April sadness

how the city of San Jose stands in my mind,
the B of A with its bell-less tower,
hot 5 P.M., walking east on Santa Clara
cross Market and First

preserved façades,
south between Second and Third
sun on car roofs, blocks
razed to keep Mexicans from crossing
(some stores left hang
banners in Vietnamese)

South of Keyes
were orchards

•

         Sunday afternoons
we drove to orchards

a grey DeSoto
or Dodge sedan, moving slowly down
gravel roads
quarter sections of trees

geometrically placed
watered

the grey Coast hills
beyond

Visitors, we parked
in front of a small barn,
were allowed to walk in among the trees,
reached into our hands & mouths
Santa Clara plums, a sweet
green fig, ripe apricots.
Our friend gave us balsa cartons
to take fruit back to the City.

·

Catherine came
to San Jose as Superior
of the convent, her last assignment.
12 years she had been Superior of the Order.

At her funeral mass Gerald said
(in his homily)
she was not one of the foolish virgins
nor would she have been one of the "sensible" virgins
either, refusing oil to her foolish sisters,
telling them to go downtown and buy some

She would have been in the Lord's house already
placing a glass of ginger ale or a cookie
in the room of each one arriving home late

as she came to the side door
of the Hayes St. convent in San Francisco
with wax paper sandwiches
of cabbage & mashed potato
for men who lined up
in the Depression.

·

Catherine entered the Sisters
of the Holy Family in 1930.
the Order, since 1872,
patronized by Irish banks, established
day homes for children of
poor: in San Jose,
cannery workers.

The fruit
left by train. The trees
sucked the water out of the ground
& it left as fruit. Water in a well
(Santa Clara & Delmas)
150 ft. (1950).

The sisters lived in underheated
California baroque luxury (mahogany paneling).

Sr. Thomasine held me as a child.

Last year, Sr. Daniel, her sister, served
shrimp salads, steaks, rolls, ice cream & coffee
to Catherine & me
in the Superior's dining room.

These people are still alive
& live on St. Elizabeth's Drive
in San Jose (& they are dead & live in this poem
with the often repetitive movements of the dead,
drawing in a skirt, just so, as to be remembered
in rooms filled with spring sunlight
& my mother's spotless furniture.

•

Leaving the convent, dazed, dazzled
by goodness I'd go back to the Holiday Inn
generously contemptuous of the ones who ate avocado
salads in the Hawaiian coffee shop or played
video games in the black alcove

& on leaving the Inn
walk up Almaden
past the offshore banks
(the orchards burnt and dozed
when electronics came)

think of recent Santa Clara grads
hoping to retain the software concession,
steal the yup trade from Mountain View, fill the new
Civic Center with suits, music, beds of flowers, & sprinklers!

•

In the old day homes
these virgins were my mothers.
I was treated
as poor.

On the polished hardwood floor
rolling in play pants. In black habit
& stiff white coif
Thomasine bends to offer
penuché on a glass plate. Downstairs,
admitted to the work areas, the stone-floored kitchen,
Sr. Malachy supervising,
two Spanish women baking,

door open on a walled garden,
a red or yellow watering can, geraniums,
tall bending stalks of snapdragon.

Catherine remembers me asking questions.
"Is it all right?" "No." (My mother's voice.)
"Is it all wrong?" Nuns smiling. One eternal
moment the content of the other, as we sit,
talking.

Raft

On the raft, floating down
whatever flows, Huck & Jim
close at the centre,
one facing upstream, trying not to remember,
feels the pressure
of the other's shoulders, facing down

remembering
boardinghouses, communes, bars,
working in offices & mills,
weddings & funerals & wakes

sitting smoking behind a barn
(or was that a story?)
sitting in the bleachers at ball games,
riding in cars, once over a bumpy field
in Gordon's Buick

sex . . .
a lobster dinner . . .

I thought I knew those places.
They were the world, each one,
mountains beyond mountains, kingdoms,
wisdom & shining gold, territory,
& there was a mother, a lover, a future.

Now this raft goes faster & faster
& I hold in my mind a map
that is the map of the world

& at my back my other
watches the islands come swooping
past, & feels my back
warm against his, his precious one.

Death Thing

I'm waiting for the bus
by the Safeway parking lot
(where George Little had his mill
in 1911, give or take a thousand years),

& I'm thinking about this death thing,
how it's outside any context
you can imagine, even one
it's self-identical with, the only item,

but how in thinking of it
we try to place it in a context
so it'll go away. Like the World Series.

•

I'm waiting for the plane.
I'm halfway through the metal detector.
I can see the mountains,
a small plane landing,

hear Tom Mackay in the bar last night, joking:
"I have no fear of flying. Crashing, yes!"
Norma broke up. We all broke up, laughing dutifully,
in respect for his bravado.

•

I'm in the Cloud Room, on the 11th floor
of the Hotel Camlin, asking my brother Gerald,

"Who did this to Seattle? Wiped out the street life,
the bars & greasy spoons on 1st Ave. & Pike
that fed Ft. Lewis soldiers in the Korean War
& us in the '60s?" He said, "Committees."

That grizzled vomit had to go.
They wanted a tasteful place to live their deaths.
They rebuilt quick, condos, afraid
those Ft. Lewis soldiers might come back,
climb up out of the excavations, snake past
the darkened construction fences, in the guise
of street kids. They did.

"It isn't even an intelligent game," I said,
"but it's not a simple one either. It's politics,
keeping people in the dark, & like all games,
it runs out. Shit happens."

·

I'm in a motel in San Francisco.
Leafing through a business magazine, I come across
an interview with an old high-school buddy,
now sits on many boards.

"Sometimes," Gordon says, "I forget the motion
when the time comes to vote."

                    Sometimes
I forget the motion, looking out the window,
thinking of contexts.

·

Hard to get my head around it,
no way to get my head around it,
my head's in it, I'm headed for it.
It'd be life I'd have to get
my head around, if anything.

"To learn that there is no Santa Claus
is perhaps the beginning of religion."
Get your head around that, get real.

This context-bound reality you construct,
this facing up to death is just the fading
of the real sense of reality, fading
of the individual. We don't "have to believe"
the world is for the young; it just is.

The Set

Remembering how it felt
working on the *Grape*
in '72, doing layout
in a grey former grocery
on Powell – we'd take a break
at suppertime & head for the pub,
knock back six or eight draft,
a package or two of chips,
maybe a pickled sausage,
& tell the waiter,
"Take one for yourself."

We were a part of history
in our mental spotlight, drinking beer
with trade unionists from the '30s,
in that battered pub (soon to be closed,
renovated & turned into a fern bar).
They told us tales
of struggles of the past.

We'd troop back, half-lit
through snowy darkness or summer shadow
to that grey, dingy, dimly lit
former grocery, to finish our layout.
There was never enough liner
or blades for the X-Acto knives & the
typeset "corrections" always came late
from the *Peak* & had to be pasted
in by hand, but the beer in our heads
kept us going past midnight – also the link
with the old union guys – with the dirty '30s –
we were for real – & we were dirty.

Do you miss all that? Do you miss the dirty '70s?
That sense there was a world & meaning
outside your mind? Tho sceptic Ed Dorn
said "the set," you could account
not just for the world but for nature itself:
the trees that leafed in the spring on Powell St.,
the stars – for you thought,
why would there be stars if there were
no world for them to shine on?

& by the third or fourth draft
your hangover would lift
& there'd be the sacred streets, in long
purple & orange stripes of sunset
to the eternal horizon,

& you called yourself a cadre,
a little yeast cell, making
tiny, correct changes in people's
consciousness, getting the paper out
on the streets. Miss all that?

I shot up to Rupert for no reason
like a steel ball in a Bally machine,
banging around the pink bumpers,
racking up points for god knows who or what.

I came almost to a stop, poised at the entrance
to one of those long, gently raked, steel alleys
you can roll down for years, decades, & still
be far from the flippers. Then I missed the world,
the beery romance of politics,
(the whiskey romance of poetry),
the set.

The Berlin Wall

Why, now that it's breached, broken, does it cause
such consternation in me?

               CBC brings me
the cries of happy youth, the singing, people
climbing up on the now meaningless Wall,
drinking champagne –

             I see myself,
eighteen months ago at Checkpoint Charlie,
hurrying across the street to avoid
the grisly American museum –

              In the narrow corridor,
slipped my Canadian passport under glass to the unsmiling
visor-capped uniformed young official – he inserts a visa,
passes it back – a loud buzzer sounds, a door swings open
into the next holding-pen – exchange West marks for East marks,
another buzzer, another door – a block or so of speed bumps &
barriers to control cars –

             then on Friedrichstrasse I stand,
an official, legal visitor to the Deutsche Demokratische Republik,
approved museum-goer, café patron, *flâneur* . . .

The past is a prison I long for, the past is a holding-pen,
the past is eternity because I did not die then.
Now youth breaks out of Kreuzberg & Wedding, out of Pankow
on the east side (side no longer), flows unchecked
across the border, smashes the rest of the broken wall even,
to widen the space
             & something in my old heart

wants to stop it, wants to retain
the orderly street, the fading State
offices, gilt-scrolled windows, resembling
banking rooms, that defined my ordinary
middle-aged eternity, my stroll, wants to
put the Wall back. As if time would stop,

as if when I went to Vancouver next week there might
be a Wall, a part of the city I could not enter except
by passing through the approved crossing-point (Broadway & Clark),
answering personal questions, giving bona fides of my existence, then
   emerging
on the far side, the good side, the dream side,
knowing myself to be a good citizen, inspected therefore
respected, & that the State (either of them) would protect me
from death.

If the young can be kept from knowing their power
(which is the power of time), if they can be made to accept
the reigning system, one memo, one regulation at a time,
with its bullshit rationale, then the old will not die.

Then the old will walk the streets of Vancouver & Berlin
fed by the respect that is paid to them by the State,
by the faces in their mirrors, & by the young, too,
unwitting collaborators, lured, conned, into the plan,

the plan behind all plans, the plan to control time.
We need not die (though we are very old), & you may remain
children, adult children. One more decade, one more year of
eternity . . .

But the reasons wear thin. Become disconnected from the
hours of the day. And the night. The places where assent had been given
are unattended.

A detour is found. The young see each other, not pictures
of the old. Then the Wall falls. One less memory is real, one patch of ground
liberated. And the old must learn that history

is not their house. They must learn, like the young,
to live by their wits.

For Prince George

I'll listen to the news the day I die,
to hear who was elected, & if
the New Jersey Devils won the sixth game
of the Stanley Cup –
not because I care about these things
(truly I care less & less),
but the game is worth the candle,
lit by the candle.

At Christmas, when lovers' eyes meet over the candles,
their thought is not "you," it's pure meaning,
infinite horizon. I'd rather be a spectator.
I'd rather be a spectator than play games.
I'd like my mind to be dumb as a lover's.

Late at night the middle-aged play Monopoly.
One spills a drink. Slurred voices,
a peal of laughter. Like the old
balls & wreaths on the tree, that dully gleam
from the darkened living room, their thoughts
come out again, sure of welcome.

Three Chinese Men

The poet: one who constantly
thinks of something else.
– Czeslaw Milosz

The three Chinese men, one with
Walkman earphones, passed by the window
of the Greek restaurant on Broadway –

no connection with the poet eating lamb chops,
facing away from the window, toward the bar,
where the owner kept appearing, a smile,
a hint of a question, on his broad face –
Is everything – is your drink – all right?

A fake marble fountain was gurgling,
a bouzouki tape played, the only other
people in the restaurant a young couple,
the girl Asian, the boy white, who seemed
to have just met & were talking softly but
continuously, as if fearful of shared silences –
A blind date? the poet thought, & then unaccountably
turned to look over his shoulder
out at whatever was there – air, wires,
buildings, a street (Broadway),
cars traveling at great speeds, & thought,
It's meaningless (as had become his wont
since attaining high office in the Party),

but looked a little longer,

& then, from his left, along the sidewalk,
conversing (well, two of them conversing,

the other had Walkman earphones),
three Chinese men. How could there be
men in a no-world? What was the one, the tall one,
saying to the other, & the third, slightly ahead,
what was he listening to? Beethoven?
Chinese opera? They passed by.

In all this nothing that surrounds you,
there was once something, there was mystery,
you didn't know what it was, it was all the more real
for your not knowing.

Then you got it down pat, you got it
fixed in your mind, you knew how to use it,
enter it. You went in & out of it, around the back,
first, where the discards were, then in the front door.
You were it, and it was you, too.

Then it began to disappear, as you will disappear,
poet, eating your Greek food. The owner
comes forward, still a bit hesitant.
"A little ouzo with your coffee, sir?"

Union Hall

If the old are allowed to be young,
the young must consent to be old.

The actual time in Ireland must be
23rd century.
So far in the future to remove
the apparent present
into the deep past.

The flat façades & the shields of the breweries,
the housefronts painted the softest of hues,
yellow & blue, pink & redpurple,
but at dusk all Irish houses are grey.

The pub is a cell of joy,
honey-whiskey light & smoke,
& narrative hilarity,
& truly, no other life
's available.

A Trip in Ireland

A poet among poets – one of the poets – with James & Jim, Dennis
O'Driscoll & Philip Casey. One of many poets – one of all who are here –
this one of all of us. No trepidation here in Ireland (look that up). No fear
of the moment, the time (now) is safe in the past. Our deaths are after, not
now. This moment is always (& always) reclaimed by the symbolic, by the
falling of words into place (like dominoes?) – like leaves. The words carry
the urgency, shoulder it, it's their own. The soul is relieved ("My burden is
light"), & the body lies down, laved in the *river of life*, with just the sense
organs protruding. Like a hippopotamus.

& what is lost, if everything is not compulsively decorated (a boy just came
to the door selling prints by Young Irish Artists), but if the walls are left
blank or a clutter of coins, ribbon & train receipts on a tray, they casually
fell too, like leaves. Nature must not be kept out at all costs as in America.
A huge crack runs the height of the window like a stem. Space left to rise
like bread. Mr. Finegan is one of the New Formalists.

So when I came here I felt sinking layer by layer – "into the bog," one
said, but it was only the companionable (Creeley's word – Irish Creeley) –
arrival at Inch – pint by pint – Kavanagh knew – how not to die –
breakfast after dark – then to Rafferty's.

Walked around Dublin Zoo – clockwise – the animals watched me, &
were quick with their tricks – the giraffe with those knobs, the cheetah
posing (no strap), bears acting Canadian, i.e., feral, like Americans back
from the wild, like Robert Bly's neo-men. "The time of men is gone,"
James proclaims, in – what was the bar? – and, "sit down, I'll get it," &
later, musing, "The ham was fine."

& the train took me, rackety-rackety, to Cork, as the elegant Killarney
woman seduced, verbally, the young North Carolina golf pro: "How many
members have you in your club?" "It's just a public links." (Look that up.)

Time doesn't all run one way. Time, too, has a geography, has caves, & you can climb down into time using only your naked toes & fingers & carry a small light bulb in a wire cage on a string around your neck, & that is sex, explosive as Miss Universe thighs or the angel in Waterstone's with the knapsack that pulled his t-shirt sleeve high on the right shoulder & his lazy rope of gold curls as he moved from Fiction to Psychology – I could not lift my eyes – I remember thinking, he's too big for me – too big for all the dark-haired, short, wide-faced aging sweating youths – & their sisters – and the odd priest with leather satchel, running to catch – & my cousin crossed himself as he neared crossings, & crossed himself as, it seems, he thought of hate or injustice – liturgical –

all the tiny bottles, the cordials, & Cadbury biscuits

"Will you have the last pint with me?" And the angel moved in & out of consciousness, still ungraspable

Arklow

The stunned faces – the stalled lives

A battle no one knows is going on (on "our" side) –
no one cares to fight. The pub a nursery,
here lessons in intricacy. But they sing Paul Simon
songs instead of the old
uprising, insurrection. Here a priest died.

Their furniture will save them. The carved & polished
& inlaid interiors of the nursery. Whispers behind
whispers. "They'll look you straight in the face
& never say a word. In Wicklow. In Wexford
people are friendlier. They'll start up a conversation
with you." Soccer its own world.

McDonald's no more invasive than Coca-Cola logos
melt in the cuban syntax, crammed & cluttered windows
& then a big, bare space. Light falling across the faces,
made for the occasion. The boy telling the man,
agitated; the man listens, arms folded, his right
hand to his chin, pensive. All history stops here,
unfolds, for a moment, its medicine chest.

Homosexuality, vegetarianism, green politics. We are
living in the dawn of the old girls' world.

9 P.M. Boys kip, men skip.

After John Newlove

I'm approaching it from the wrong direction & so I don't recognize it.
Someone – that's as basic as you can get – someone is who we are.
Someone arrived, just a moment ago, from the previous moment, where
not-he, not-she, had spent a century, an eternity, but then not-his, not-her,
lease was up, & someone had to skedaddle – & arrived here, not knowing
what it was not-she, not-he, confronted, was over against, because not-he,
not-she, approached it from the wrong direction.

If this is the world, then where am I,
what is this loneliness, this outpost?
Or if I am not I, but only someone,
then there is nothing I am over against.

Finally we all face this together,
but don't know what it is, even
though no longer approaching it, in the heart
of it, in our hearts, but still, somehow,
from the wrong direction.

From someone's heart.

Poem Enclosing Its Dedications

& now I'm looking at someone
in a t-shirt, who comes out of the shade
of his apartment & wags his fingers, briefly,
against the steel frame of his glass door
so they flash white, in the sun.

The sun makes the apartment building opposite
reflect the light, off its paint,
dirt-streaked.

Two trolley poles skim past (the top halves).
The wires sway
    for Judith Copithorne & Daniel Ignas
The hemlocks or firs or whatever move slightly
in the breeze
    for Renee Rodin

Another man in a t-shirt gets out of a grey car
(I don't know the names of things –
trees, makes of cars).
The blue sky says nothing,
but what would you expect it to say –
do you think that behind it there are wheels?

A man with a yellow shirt & a
yellow cap. A blue truck. If I don't know
him by name why should I know the truck's
family?
    for Barbara Munk

A lyric poem.
A man in a brown vest & a t-shirt

carrying a plastic Safeway bag.
The traffic signal sways.
                      The blue sky means the sun
is warming Vancouver.
                    Another bus,
this one going west, to Dunbar or UBC,
so I can see the full length of the poles.

Maroon car. Man in blue jeans & grey
sweatshirt & black helmet on a bike. Another
guy on a bike. Woman with raspberry red coat
walks up old concrete steps with a Safeway
bag.
    Red car.
Cherry red. Wild cherry.

Four people, one pushing a bike.
Green sweat, white helmet.

Man sits at desk, looks out window at
cream-coloured apartment building, parked cars,
conifers he doesn't know the name of, only
knows they're conifers cause he can remember them
greenblack in winter – at trolley wires &
thicker black (hydro?) cable, sometimes birds
sit on, crows, pigeons –

old '20s 2-storey gable-roofed house on
Trafalgar, Avalon milk truck, blue
sign of Westside Ski & pink sign of
Montri's restaurant

& blue sky all behind this. Sky blue.

Sits writing poem. Wowowow of ambulance.

Stops.

Stops writing. Poem goes on, world goes on.

Dobie (shot for poaching)

Fierce & independent as a wolf,
courteous as an urbanite,
your silence resembled the human silence
of a sea captain or explorer,
one who had seen much in more than one world.

Ripple + 26

for Ken Bullock & Philip O'Connor

26, not 20. Years. In the future. I'm sitting on the edge of my bed in a hotel room in Montreal, yes, but not examining my hands, the spots of age are there, yes, but I have no wish to examine any part of me, wish, I wish, no wish. In San Francisco I thought, & I don't care what I thought, I looked forward, I imagined, to this moment, 20, only it's 26, years, to ratify (whatever that means, turn into a rat, I guess) some notion I had of me (& the rat's loose now, behind the boards).

This is an old Victorian, a *manoir* it's called (now I have to shift over, on the bed, writing (& see my 62-year-old legs) (what was so important about not remembering someone's name (I *still* forget people's names when I get stoned) that it took me 26 years to (I'm sitting in a hotel room in Prince George trying to remember what it was so important to remember in a hotel room in Montreal about not remembering someone's name in San Francisco 26 – I forget. And the guy whose name I forgot – Tom? – now I've forgotten *him*, though Monday (last Monday (2 Mondays ago) in Vancouver, Ken Bullock told me Phil O'Connor had been asking after me, & that's longer, 47 years I guess since I've seen him, he was one of my moral mentors (*one* of?) I told Ken, taught me something about lust for power, i.e., you don't pick on 3 guys (pages, at the Main Library (Kelham, 1917)), when there's 9 of you (even if you are a sissy) – but me, me, that's important (the rat sd), I meant that isn't important (isn't it nice the way he cleans the blood off his hands before dinner (& twisted another way, so now he could see he was wearing paisley shorts, tapered boxers ("You refuse to get old" – B.G.) – I'm not as old as this *manoir* – I lost it.

It doesn't matter where you start or where you end, you're you (I'm you), not me, there is no rat (not so fast, you want to get your thoughts together, like candy eggs (the colours of the 4 Montreal subway – *métro!* – lines – blue, orange, green, yellow – in an Easter basket (& back there in San

Francisco there was something about candy too – let's face it (he sat up & faced it – curtain, window, lightwell, highrise – a false note

I'm sitting on the edge of this bed in a Montreal hotel room & there is nothing that needs to be said (o false note of closure – thanks, sd the rat, I have lots to say, & I'm driving (there is no rat)

I read poetry last night to 6 people – 3 seemed interested – not including me – I do this for myself. I'm sweating all over. I'm wearing weird brown socks (or are they gold?) with black & white squares on them. I don't want to deny what the guy 26 years back said – he said "It's all me" – it was all him – sure, the world has no mind – no one mind – there is no "world" – now that's a fact – or the lack of a fact. It isn't candy – is that a rat running cross the roof? He jumped up, pulled back the curtain all the way, looked out – it looked back, from up on the fire escape – no, not a rat, a white squirrel. Now that certainly ain't part of me, a coloured Easter egg.

Those 3 guys we were going to beat up, or "get" in some way, were library pages. Phil was one of them – the biggest one – & he came & said to me (we were standing in the doorway of the little anteroom behind the main reading room, where we pages sorted books & put them on trucks for shelving) – "What if it had been Ken?" (another Ken – a smaller boy – & he'd be over 60 now (the rat is wearing a yellow shirt – the one I wore last night at the reading – purple tie, check – & driving, driving – forget the rat). That was the first time I heard moral indignation in anyone's voice. Christ, I didn't want to hear that. That we tune out (what was so important to remember, I didn't remember someone's name? For a minute. A minute or 2. And then the Tao came back, I wrote then. I don't think I've got my thoughts very well organized here. Not like those beautiful rubber-tired subway cars.

I guess I'll just have to keep driving – writing. I guess I am the rat (ratified, finally) sitting on the real bed in the real hotel room in the real Montreal, with my half-eaten candy thoughts, & always the sickness of incomplete – just wanting to locate myself here as you rather than me. *You* know, Emily Carr said when the dark asked her why. You know. *You Who Know* (Nicolas Freeling) wanting to disappear, of course, but be here, if it takes all night, if it takes 26, 47, 62 years to put lust for power behind me.

Montreal/Prince George 1996

At Andy's

for Andy and Martina

Terrace '97. I arrive here on the bus, Andy & Martina pick me up (while I'm writing I'll try to ignore undercurrents of the brain, personal worthiness, outcome or "point" of this writing, e.g., or should I include them? A pointless paragraph. I can't write.

OK, I guess I really do have to freewrite & quit fucking around. So – dive in – splash – *in medias res* – don't like this pen, point too short – I arrive on the bus – strip mall on Keith – we stop at Safeway for groceries – obesity – almost everyone too big, I think, is the weight of all the food that gets here, by truck (less waste, and, Andy reminds me, heat loss) added to the bodies of those living here, Terraceites?

Streets jammed with cars, we take the long way up to the bench, a kid pulling away from the West Side food store drinking a Coke seems enclosed in his car – encased –

What's wrong is somehow I think there's something to write about – instead of writing.

I'm sitting down here in Andy's basement at Vicky's old desk on a hot Sunday in August thinking I should write about something, or rather, that I should (emphasize *should*) write (emphasize *write*) to justify my existence – my life – to myself (& then having justified self, I can be with others, have a drink with Andy, e.g., without feeling self-unjustified (un-self-justified?). I'm appalled – horrified – that at age 63 I still think this way – write this way. I can't write, Barry & I say. What would "writing" be? I think of the quick, sharp (objectivist) takes on heart & world in GB's *Blondes on Bikes* – I can't do that – wouldn't even try, to act so nonchalant, i.e., pretend to. I started out to write about Terrace & here I am writing about myself, with as bad a fit between this so-called writing activity (free writing – what's *free* about it?) – & content – & poetry! – as ever. I should *pray*, I guess – just keep writing this silly shit & pray for a poem.

•

White hair on the back of my hand – radio going upstairs – I go upstairs, Andy tells me about constant noise from next-door subdivision – rottweilers, dachshund – bulldozer – angry crows. I go outside, sit on porch, hear crows –

I hear crows in Vancouver – I have nothing to write about, & am not in right state to dive deep – on edge here – hate this pen – there is no content – or is age content? (Kavanagh: "they know it to a day") – fuck that – feeling myself breathe – insect makes wide sweep around flowerpot – Teddy barks –

Poetry means (a) I'm going to die – & (b) this notebook will be read by someone who will see how lacking I am – unless I destroy it – & I can't do that – that would be worse than keeping it – that would mean thinking of it. Better this shit than nothing, better be sitting on Andy's front porch with Teddy, imagining this shit being (miraculously) turned into a poem – as Spicer said, not the Vietnam War but Autumn in Vermont – a poem about obesity, cheerful obesity, all the big people trundling their carts & bags of groceries out to their cars parked at the mall – one lifestyle – nothing but the economy – the drinking water sour – environmental movement focused on the immediate, daily threats to health –

At the college – MACLABUSE, one word, becomes MACL ABUSE, a new threat? Abuse, abuse, obese – truckloads of log corpses from farther & farther away, up the Nass – operate the mill at lower cost, develop the mining sector, truckloads of food – this is a site of conversion, realization of surplus value, how else to conceive of it.

No way to conceive of it, no understanding. And I'll never know if it's really understanding that's disappearing or am I just moaning the loss of a sharper mind.

Well, I've started writing again.

•

Drinking water – foul – a sour or flat taste & then a chemical aftertaste – two-stage foulness.

Sky overcast – air muggy – due to automobiles? Is anything "natural" anymore?

This is not poetry. But what would a poem about Terrace be like? Objective – at a distance from the mind, posing as anybody's perception, idea – or no one's. The View from Nowhere. But is there another alternative? Ah, inspiration!

I wish I had a desk – I'm sitting on this duvet in Annyha's bedroom, balancing the writing book on my naked knees – I feel like I'm in the jungle. But nothing to pounce on me, except myself – always pouncing.

Fine rain, and now, to the west, a rift of blue like a river in the white cloud – blue rifts opening up over the cedars – fine rain – me here – a visitor – seeing Terrace from the outside. I was extracted – like a tooth – early retirement – & the skin of Terrace closed easily behind me, the placidity, the obesity. A feeling of contentment – & exclusion – at the edges of this the trees are eaten – the best logs hauled, the second best burned or buried – hauled back here – then the conversion begins – the logs turn into money (the computer watches the saw) – some of it stays here – & then the trucks come, the food – & also the car carriers (any name for that?), rattling & clanking, steel ramps, chains – an objective poem, no one's vision –

Cars moving slowly up Lakelse – cumbersome – in & out of parking spaces – slow – because so heavy & so dangerous – & there is food, in bags, in carts, lifted into trunks & back seats of cars, backs of pickups, in mall lot. Cars & trucks move slowly, heavily, toward the exit, then move like heavy tanks into the traffic lanes, & then, inside all this, inside the cars (the objective poem sees) there are people, placid, cheerful –

What a vision! – is there behind this some animus – is it deep dislike of these people, misanthropy, or just objective – is this a phenomenon anyone could observe or the twisted vision of a fucked-up old man – is there anything natural – or is it *all* natural – blameless – the programmed activities of sapiens with their tree trunks on trucks, wood chips in hopper cars, cars & carts & such no less than insects with sticks & leaves – each has its function, its social role.

The salt lost its savour, but is it only in my life? What is it I don't grant them, the Terraceites of '97 – the right to be fat & happy & to have overcome (not individually, but *en masse*), simply by not learning it, dread?

•

Who can see the inner Terrace? Do our individual hearts meet there as our social selves meet here in this slow-moving jumble of steel carapaces & Safeway carts & fat pleasant faces with the log trucks an undertone in the background? We aren't crowded together there, that I know. Or do we not meet? Is there a place, even in summer, where each man (& woman) moves continually away, through a personal winter, saying, "this is true"?

There's no way to know except by knowing them, which here I don't, except my old friends – & their knowledge of each other, seen in faces & heard in tones of voice more than in words – knowledge of what is not said, out of kindness – life a condition of unsaying, of waiting for the unsaid to fade, of waiting for forgetfulness while preserving shards of memory, of avoiding laying it all on each other, out of forbearance.

In Hawthorne's story "The Minister's Black Veil," the minister blames his community for their forbearance as if that were a sin of secrecy & not a balm of love – to suffer the unsaid in privacy – in one's knowledge that ultimately that's what there is – aloneness – the urge to lay it all on the other being a desperate cry, a try, at leaping that bulwark of loneness, to enforce mutual knowledge, mutual terror.

Do we consume merely out of duty, is it a façade, that we pretend to savour the objects we devour, pretend to praise the process, and these fat smiles are not of satisfaction in consuming but of living in virtue, of never revealing, of ever concealing, the true life we know the other also lives – in darkness, in winter?

•

(At Mr. Mike's)

I can't separate my feelings from their faces. If I could peel them back like a film, from the fat & placid – huge man ordering grapefruit juice – "on a diet" – what would they seem?

They would seem nothing – their faces are in my mind – that's not solipsism, just Terrace-ism. I sit in Mr. Mike's – the veggie burger & Coke – a sketch in the brain –

•

(On the Halliwell bus)

The bus driver said of one of his passengers: "When she started riding the bus she wouldn't say a word. You'd ask her a question & she'd give you just a little short answer. But now . . ." (Pause.) "She's a Christian, her parents brought her up to be a Christian – but I told her, hey, I don't hold it against you, & she gave a little laugh."

By which they know how they feel – she knows he didn't mean to dis her faith – but they say so little – "she wouldn't say a word" means a feeling that could be explained in other words, shy, or frightened even, but the driver doesn't –

Maybe the bus driver knows why she wouldn't say a word – abuse – but won't say, maybe because he's protecting her – from a word, spoken out loud, to a stranger – to me – "I haven't seen you on this bus before" –

Feelings are there in the air, in the mind – "this side of the grass" we walk among feelings – & carry feelings in our brains – & so the faces act as doors – set in lines – not to let words in. Words dart about inside, puckish – Andy's father asked what that word meant – mischievous, *méchant* – up to no good – words, like spirits, neither good nor evil, just natural – but some would call them good *and* evil – Christians – so the faces –

•

Who am I, a ghost? Walking up from Greig to Lakelse – one of those streets east of Kalum – empty lots & broken house foundations – weeds – think, am I here – am I a ghost? I'm not here, not in the sense that thoughts & feelings & the odd word (at the joint – words at the joints) would carry me – to the next meeting – I could be going to a meeting (come in late, like Ken Belford) – for city politics or to get drunk or for sex – yes, many of those meanings – meetings – but no network –

& love & courage, Simon Thompson said, at the bar, at Hanky's – we had met there every year & now were meeting again – Rocque, José, Andy – those narratives, Simon said, are somehow replaced or annihilated – by consumer –

Happy to read an account of Margaret Laurence's suicide – her own account – she couldn't find the teakettle to heat the water to melt the Diazepam – tranquilizer, Andy says, like Prozac – so she used the coffeemaker, but didn't put any coffee – just hot water & Prozac – & the glinting memory – faces of joy – one last?

·

Dream poem: tyler alters / night amber / with sensation.

·

The same world for me as for Andy – we agree. Not the Thing-in-Itself – that horror-movie creature – but a thing between us and the Thing – something we have made up (using all our unspoken language) – call it world. So how is it I stand in it, on the broken asphalt & concrete sidewalks of Terrace, & feel it not – feel it *as* not – as departure, Rilke might say? At Andy's I feel part of it, hearing Andy's lawnmower, seeing the grey pile rug & blond dresser in Annyha's room, two pairs of my shoes – writing at 3:15 P.M. – it feels like I'm here, & that I won't leave.

The world that seems so frightening (admit it) when smoking dope (it's the fright I'm admitting, not the dope) or when thinking – too rationally – you could sit on the porch – *and* imagine it – stars coming on in the 10-o'clock evening, maybe Orion, time of year? – but chill, too early for stars to come out fully – late by the clock, but too early for the meteor shower – Andy's voice from the dark, down by the barn – "take 15 or 20 minutes longer, but I'm not waiting, I'm going to bed." "Me too."

Located in it – not located – in it – not in it – it – not it – I? – no, not I –
the? The the (Barry's line, from Wallace Stevens). The with stars.

●

Old Lakelse Lake Road – driving to John & Larisa's for dinner. I'm
holding the dessert in my lap – a cake – & Martina in front of me holds a
bowl of caramel sauce. Andy drives. Dark sky – scattered rain – second-
growth cedars packed in – roadside bushes – branches waving in the wind
– I watch the raindrops crawl up the windshield & I feel the void, like a
natural phenomenon, stabbing out of the clouds, or flashing without light
– but alternating – on & off – with its absence – something more
substantial? – faith?

In Ireland

1   The Dying Cow

My father appeared to me, or rather,
appeared in me, as I was sitting at the bar
in a pub in Wicklow called The Dying Cow.
Appeared in me, shoulder in my shoulders,
lips in my lips, in that attitude
of resignation that marked his old age.

I realized I had long warded him off,
looked in the mirror countless times
& saw my short hair sticking up like his
    from my age-high brow
& quickly brushed it to the side;
felt my lips purse in that small mouth of his
that could not kiss (but admired kissing)
& more & more as he grew old would not
speak, knowing what he had to say would be
of no importance.
               I would be gay, I would
(pretend to) kiss. His anger, in childhood,
    had propelled me outward,
to seek a world where to be what he was not,
whatever that might be, might be wanted –
not learned, because I though I had it in me –
some secret soul yet daunted by his look,
    by his repeated rebuke,
horrified that I might be that way.

How far I ran from him to discover a place
    (New York)
where I could finally begin. Combed my hair
to let it fall over my brow, widened, with effort,
my smile. Especially in snapshots.

I am trying to tell all this too quickly,
as if the right word (that might come to me
as I thought my soul would come to me
as a teenager, breaking away from him) might tell
some truth about us. About him & me.

2   Coolgreany Wood

Thoughts of death walking through old oak wood
much of which had been cut for furniture.
Look at a space between branches: no world,
nothing surrounding, clouds indifferent.

Odd affection for the openness of that sky –
Felt his co-presence sharp again within me –
This time it was the universe's turn
    to say nothing.

Veracruz

In Veracruz, city of breezes & sailors & loud birds,
an old man, I walked the Malecón by the sea,

and I thought of my father, who when a young man
had walked the Malecón in Havana, dreaming of Brazil,

and I wished he had gone to Brazil
& learned magic,

and I wished my father had come back to San Francisco
armed with Brazilian magic, & that he had married
not my mother, but her brother, whom he truly loved.

I wish my father had, like Tiresias, changed himself into a woman,
& that he had been impregnated by my uncle, & given birth to me as a girl.

I wish that I had grown up in San Francisco as a girl,
a tall, serious girl,

& that eventually I had come to Veracruz,
& walking on the Malecón, I had met a sailor,
a Mexican sailor or a sailor from some other country –
    maybe a Brazilian sailor,
& that he had married me, & I had become pregnant
    by him,
so that I could give birth at last to my son – the boy
    I love